Colonial Cadet in Nigeria

Colonial Cadet in Nigeria

John Smith

Number 34 in a series published for the
Duke University Commonwealth-Studies Center
Duke University Press, Durham, N. C.
1968

Printed in the United States of America
by Kingsport Press, Inc., Kingsport, Tennessee

Author's Note

The work and life of British administrators in colonial Northern Nigeria in the early years of the century is well documented. Little has been written since that is generally available, and the interesting period immediately prior to independence has inevitably and rightly been studied from the viewpoint of the Nigerian nationalist rather than from that of the British official.

This book recalls my first five years in Northern Nigeria. I was appointed as a cadet in 1951, the last year of large-scale British recruitment to the Nigerian Administrative Service, which was to be so recklessly and needlessly dispersed a decade later. As my sources I have used diaries, correspondence, and official reports which I wrote at the time. Some of the official reports are included at the end of the book. My object has been simple: to show the kind of men we were and the type of work the majority of us, at the broad base of the administrative pyramid, did, and how we did it.

I am as deeply involved in Nigeria now as I was at the time about which I write. The Colonial Service was an involving career. I do not therefore profess to be objective, but I have tried to be both frank and critical. There was plenty wrong with the service and with Northern Nigeria. It could all have been so much better, but it might have been very much worse. I arrived in a relatively developed country just as great changes were to occur. It was soon a difficult race to keep ahead of events. But we managed, and that we did so was due to those who had served before us, with more leisure but less comfort, laying the administrative foundations of a nation, accomplishing so much in so short a time. My respect for their achievement is great. I doubt if any group of men could have done better.

I am indebted to Mr. Robert Heussler who suggested the project, and to Professor Taylor Cole, Dr. W. B. Hamilton, and others of Duke University who made its execution possible.

Durham, North Carolina, May, 1967

Contents

Glossary of Government and Civil Service Structure

Region	The component parts of the Federation of Nigeria as established on October 1, 1954.
Province	An administrative unit within a region.
Division	An administrative unit within a province.
Township	An urban administrative unit equal in status to a division and administered directly by government.
Emirate	The domain of an emir, the usual title of a Moslem chief in Northern Nigeria.
District	An administrative unit within an emirate.
Village	An administrative unit within a district.
Hamlet, Ward	Administrative units within a village.
Governor-General	In 1951 Nigeria had a Governor and three Chief Commissioners in the Northern, Eastern, and Western Provinces. In 1952 the Chief Commissioners became Lieutenant-Governors. In 1954 the creation of a Federation made the Governor a Governor-General, and the Lieutenant-Governors full Governors. It can be seen that the path to independence was not without its rewards for British officials!
Resident	The senior government official in a province.
SDO	Senior District Officer, the title of an administrative officer, next in rank to a Resident and in charge of the more important divisions.
DO	District Officer
ADO	Assistant District Officer, the rank obtained after three years probationary service.
Cadet	The most junior administrative officer, unconfirmed in his appointment and on probation for three years.

Prime Minister, Premier	The head of government of the Federation was called the Prime Minister and the heads of government in the Regions were known as Premiers.
Minister	The title for a member of the government, whether federal or regional.
Native Authority	The local government body responsible for an emirate, usually composed of an emir and his council. Abbreviated to NA.
Emir	The title of a Moslem chief in the Hausa states. Other chiefly titles were in use elsewhere.
District Head	The NA official in charge of a district. Abbreviated to DH.
Village Head	The NA official in charge of a village. Abbreviated to VH.
Hausa titles	Most senior officials of a Native Authority are known by their traditional titles, *Waziri, Ciroma, Madaki,* etc., rather than by their own names. Titles are conferred by an emir and are an indication of a man's standing in the community.

Colonial Cadet in Nigeria

Prologue

As a boy my first love was the sea. Imperfect vision reconciled me at the age of fourteen to a life ashore, but did not destroy my hope of adventure and a career out of doors. A Christmas holiday's avid reading of antarctic exploration settled me on surveying as the means to this end. Then, in my last year at school, my mother chanced on a careers exhibition. She brought home a bundle of booklets, among them Rex Niven's *A Day in the Life of a District Officer*. This worked upon my dislike of math and increasing satisfaction in history. I exchanged surveying for administration and Antarctica for Africa.

The war ended and I went up to University College, London, to read history, specializing in Latin-American independence. Asked at the Colonial Service Appointments Board interview why I had not studied British colonial history, I rather glibly replied that I had thought it more valuable to understand why Spain had lost an empire than to know how Britain had gained one. This didn't go down very well, and a member of the board, who turned out to be a former governor of British Honduras, proceeded to quiz me very shrewdly. I was rescued by a jovial north-countryman, who must have been a trade union representative, for this was in the days of the postwar Labour government. Knowing that I had been in Egypt he asked me how the pyramids had been built. Without giving me an opportunity to reply, he proceeded to tell me, using up the rest of the interview time to the consternation of the chairman and obvious irritation of his colleagues.

A few weeks later I got home from a glorious summer day's sailing to find a telegram informing me of my appointment and allocation to Nigeria. It was not until October, when I went up to Oxford to attend the Devonshire Course and found Hausa on the syllabus, that I knew I was destined for the Northern rather than the Southern Provinces. While Rex Niven's booklet had fostered my interest in colonial administration, it had decided me against the area of which he wrote, and to which I was now assigned. Subsequent military service in the Middle East had convinced me that turbanned emirs and hawk-eyed wazirs were not my idea of Africa. I fancied something less traditional and more direct. But I was pleased enough to have a job at all, and looking around me at home began to realize that Northern Nigeria had long since played a part in my life, albeit less than Tanganyika where I was nearly born and which had been my choice of territory. My father had served in Nigeria, as a bachelor, from 1912 to 1922 before his service in East Africa. There had always been a Hausa Bible on the bookshelves, and now I pulled out a volume of Hausa folk stories with interest. A family seaside home had been called *Sai Anjima*[1] in deference to inevitable family separation, and although Swahili predominated in our family language, we had borrowed a little from Hausa. I poured over old photograph albums and my mother dug out letters written years before. Not only did the country to which I was going become alive but also my father, who had been killed in an early African air accident when I was six years old.

Professor Heussler's archetype of *Yesterday's Rulers*[2] had been much diluted by 1950, the last year of really large-scale recruitment by the Colonial Office into the West African services. The thirty of us who assembled at Oxford destined for Northern Nigeria were all ex-servicemen but not all ex-officers, and by no means all graduates. Many, like myself, had had a grammar school education. London and the civic universities were as well represented as Oxbridge. The myth of the public school and Oxbridge man was real enough however. I doubt if any of my schoolmasters really thought I'd make it, and certainly an official of the University of London Appointments Board told me bluntly that London graduates didn't stand a chance.

1. The Hausa farewell, meaning until we meet again.
2. Robert Heussler, *Yesterday's Rulers* (Syracuse, N. Y.: Syracuse University Press, 1963) is an account of the making of the British Colonial Service.

The year at Oxford was a pleasant interlude but of little training and even less academic value. A London graduate, perhaps I smarted too much at Oxford's refusal to recognize my degree and consequent treatment as a freshman *in statu pupilari*. But I also found the caliber of teachers and teaching much below that to which I had been accustomed in undergraduate days at UCL. Three things redeemed the course. We began to learn Hausa and received a grammatical basis which was to be useful when we came into daily contact with the language. We had leisure and facilities to read up on Nigeria and slowly work ourselves in. Finally, the Colonial Service Club, under the genial guidance of Jerry Cornes, the course supervisor, was a cheerful and friendly place to meet future colleagues attending the senior course or visiting on leave. Once a week one of these would be prevailed upon to talk to us informally and informatively about the aspects of the job or country which seemed of most interest to him. One other abiding memory of Oxford is warding off insurance salesman ready to quote special terms for the "white man's grave"! Those of us who have since been involved with the training of our African successors now realize how much better it might all have been. As an induction the Devonshire Course was far too extravagant of time and much too imprecise in detail, while the academic standing of some of those associated with the course did not compensate for low standards in too wide a field.

From our senior colleagues and visitors we learned enough as time went by to decide to which province we would like to be posted. To me far and away the most exciting prospect was Adamawa with its touring stations at Mubi, Jada, and on the Mambilla Plateau. My disappointment was great when on May 21 I learned of my posting to Kano. But time rushed by as we busied ourselves with the tropical outfitters, and postings we had heard were often changed. On July 12 we set sail from Liverpool in the m.v. "Apapa." Our future responsibilities began to make themselves felt. The Emir of Gombe, whom we had met at Oxford, was a fellow passenger. His traveling companion suffered from seasickness, so we took it in turns to keep the Emir company and practice our Hausa. We were somewhat surprised on arrival in

Lagos to find that secretariat officers were not particularly interested in "our" Emir.

Sir John Macpherson was governor when we arrived and an innovator in staff matters. His "new look" allowed us a rushed three-day introduction to Lagos, the capital, something previously regarded as unnecessary, and by some Northern officials, no doubt, as unwise. We were all guests of administrative officers. I found myself tasting for the first time (and last as a cadet) the luxury of gracious living at the top, for I was entertained by the Chief Secretary. The fine and spacious house beautifully situated on the lagoon, the crisp, efficient, and silent servants who laundered any garment discarded in a matter of minutes, the good table, and the charm of our host and hostess were the only side of the Colonial Service that Members of Parliament, Whitehall civil servants, and foreign correspondents ever saw. Most of them forgot that they were enjoying the merited rewards of an able few after long service in very different conditions.

Like most newcomers to the coast, I found the lateness of the dinner hour the major problem I faced in what is now known as "cultural shock." My second evening I and some others were invited to dine with a bachelor officer of the old school. He still drove to his office by pony and trap and he never called for dinner before eleven. Initiating us into the mysteries of palm-oil chop, he insisted on testing the consistency of the pounded yam by tossing it up into the revolving ceiling fan. It failed the test, and to our dismay the table was cleared and the cook ordered to start again.

We did not realize how novel our mode of induction was, and we certainly did not have the proper sense of awe when invited to Government House to meet Northern officers working in Lagos. Two incidents remain clearly in my mind. A rather fierce Scotswoman, the wife of a Resident, took me aside and said: "Young man, never, never refer to monkeynuts in this country. We call them groundnuts." HE, as we had already learned to call the Governor, although a sick man, had us up one by one for a chat. He asked me how long a career I thought lay before me. "A certain five years, a probable ten, and a lucky fifteen," I replied.

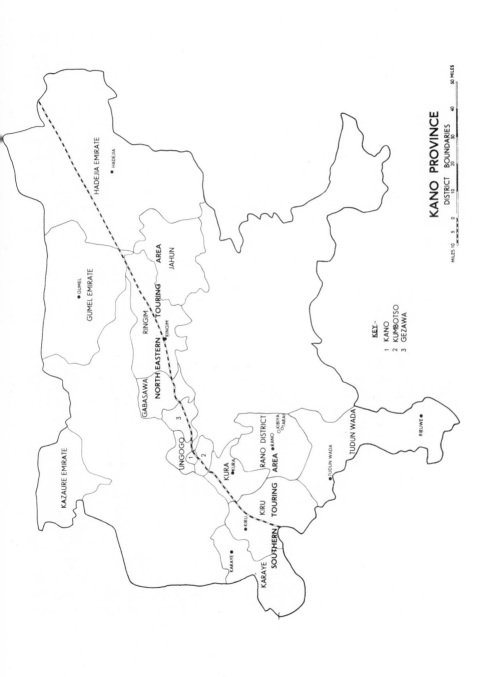

KANO PROVINCE

KAZAURE EMIRATE

GUMEL EMIRATE
• GUMEL

HADEJIA EMIRATE
• HADEJIA

GABASAWA

RINGIM
• RINGIM

NORTH EASTERN TOURING AREA

JAHUN

UNGOGO
1
2
3

KURA
• KURA

RANO DISTRICT
• KIBIYA
O TARAI
• RANO

RANO TOURING AREA

TUDUN WADA
• TUDUN WADA

• RIBUWE

KIRU
• KIRU

KARAYE
• KARAYE

SOUTHERN TOURING AREA

KEY:-
1 KANO
2 KUMBOTSO
3 GEZAWA

DISTRICT BOUNDARIES

MILES 10   5   0   10   20   30   40   50 MILES

LAKE CHAD

BENUE

RIVER

TERRITORY

TRUST

CAMEROONS

NIGERIA   1950

MILES 80 40 0   80   160   240   320   400 MILES

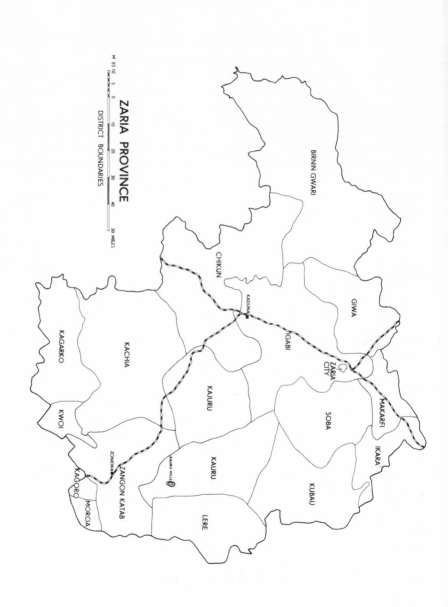

ZARIA PROVINCE

DISTRICT BOUNDARIES

MILES 10 5 0   10   20   30   40   50 MILES

BIRNIN GWARI

CHIKUN

GIWA

KADUNA

IGABI

ZARIA CITY

MAKARFI

KAGARKO

KACHA

KAJURU

SOBA

IKARA

KWOI

KAURU

KUBAU

KAGORO

ZANGON KATAB

KAURU HILLS

LERE

MOROA

ZONKWA

"My boy," he said, patting me on the knee, "you have thirty years or more ahead of you. My own son is coming into the service next year."

I certainly went to Nigeria not only aware of nationalist demands for self-government (1956 was then the favored date) but sympathetic to them. I accepted the concepts of the "dual mandate" and "indirect rule" in the context of independence as the objective and a belief in racial equality. The few African students I had known came from Nigeria or the Gold Coast, among them Kwame Nkrumah, whose political yearnings I listened to one night in a Tottenham Court Road pub. I had heard with respect and approval Sir Francis Ibiam, a member of the Nigerian Legislative Council, talking to us at Oxford of his country's aspirations. What was true of me was true of a number of my colleagues, but the mechanics of our job as junior officers and of our life as Europeans in an African country mattered more to us than political speculation. In any case I soon realized that many of my seniors, lacking my postwar student experience, might not share my views. When, for example, Sir Francis Ibiam's talk was published in the nationalist press, colleagues in Kano were shocked that the Colonial Office had allowed such an occasion to take place. Student Union activities and soldiering as a temporary officer (and regarded a temporary gentleman too by some of the regulars) had taught me diplomacy. I kept my counsel. There was so much to learn in my new job and I seemed so remote from the lofty peaks of power that I paid little or no attention to national politics in my first tour. I had no radio and was only rarely able to buy newspapers. Above all, the mass of the people among whom I worked were neither involved nor interested.

We caught the train north, slowly shedding colleagues on the forty-two-hour journey to Kano. I went sick with malaria, the result presumably of a stray mosquito from a home-going ship biting me at Las Palmas. On arrival I spent three days in a hospital. The man acting in charge of Kano Division then took me in hand, and could not have been kinder. Nor could anyone have fitted more perfectly the district officer of imagination. Tall and handsome, he loved the life, and everyone, responding to his natural sympathy, loved him. He worked extremely hard, played all games well, and lived in the romantic *Gidan Dan Hausa*,[3] a house with three-foot-thick mud walls and a thirty-foot-high domed dining room. From him I learned much in the few days allowed me to sort out my kit, buy a horse, and find a servant before setting out on my first eighteen months as a colonial cadet.

3. *Gida* is Hausa for house. *Dan Hausa,* meaning son of a Hausaman, was the nickname of Hans Vischer, a renowned Hausa speaker and an early educator of vision. *Gidan Dan Hausa* had been his house. It stands today, an ancient monument, and a memorial to the first British officers in Kano.

Part 1. Touring Officer,
Kano Division

In July, 1951, although on the brink of a series of constitutional changes which were to lead to independence, Nigeria was still governed as a unitary territory on more or less the traditional pattern of colonial administration. The provincial administration of Kano consisted of a senior Resident, a Resident, a senior district officer in charge of Kano Division with some eight to ten junior administrative officers helping him, and a district officer and one assistant in the Northern Division. I was sent to Kazaure, a small emirate in Kano Division, to learn at first hand how a native authority worked. The DO who lived in the Kazaure touring area was an excellent Hausa speaker and possessed of a sharp sense of humor. His improper asides to me in English in conversations with the elderly and far from clean Emir made it difficult to take seriously this initiation into the mystique of indirect rule. As in most native authorities one man really mattered, in this case the *Magajin Gari,* warm friend of many a British officer and later to be the most successful of the provincial commissioners when the post of Resident was made political.[1] I noticed that with him my DO had a very different relationship built upon mutual respect for ability and integrity.

A letter to my mother described my resthouse, a standard pattern in which I was to spend so much time in the next few years. Local building, except for houses of the rich, was round, and resthouses were likewise round mud buildings with a grass thatch. The European refinement was an outer round wall of half height providing a veranda. The inner room was always dark and often bat-infested. Most of us put our kit into it and set up our

1. In 1962 ministers were appointed with the portfolio of a province to replace residents, who were civil servants.

bed, table and chair, and bath around the veranda. I commented that the resthouse was, according to my DO, "exceptionally well furnished. There is a table, a chair, and a stool."

My own touring equipment consisted of a camp bed and bedding, a folding table, a folding chair, a canvas washbasin and bath, a latrine seat, a pressure lamp, pots and pans and a mincer for the kitchen, crockery, cutlery, and linen for the table. There was little difference between my household belongings and those of earlier administrators. Hastings, who went to Nigeria in 1906, described his furniture as consisting "of a camp bed, small wooden table, long canvas chair, and a small folding one . . . a canvas folding bath and washing basin, a heavy square lantern, called a 'Lord's Lamp,' and a square of rubber ground sheet, and that was all."[2]

I grew very fond of my camp kit during those early months, and perhaps only those who have experienced it can understand how homely I felt sitting by a small table with whisky bottle and soda syphon, pipe and tobacco, and a book in the mellow hissing light of a kerosene lamp. My bed was always beautifully made with that variety of fancy turndown patterns for top sheet and blanket of which the West African servant is master, and encased in the snug security of a net, proof against bats, scorpions, and lizards as well as mosquitoes. Beside it was a locally woven grass mat, and on top of the cash box at the head of the bed stood a glass and water in an empty Gordon's gin bottle. In truth I lived comfortably. I ate off china, drank from good glass, and had a clean starched napkin at every meal. I always traveled with a gramophone and records and a box of books. But it wasn't the luxury depicted in some novels and about which I had heard angry comments from West African students in England. Refrigerators, for example, were only about this time becoming a standard government issue, and it was two years before I possessed one.

New arrivals were taught how to live by their servants, who were usually inherited on promotion from a senior colleague.

2. A. C. G. Hastings, *Nigerian Days* (London: Bodley Head, 1925), p. 37.

Mine, Buba, was a DO's second steward and had been an officers' mess servant in Burma during the war. Like most of the old-time servants he had begun as a ball boy in a tennis club and graduated from this to servant's servant, to small boy, and so on up the ladder to head steward. Times were changing. Buba could cook as well as valet. He became my cook-steward and we took on as second a huge and cheerful kinsman for the princely sum of 7s. a week.

At Kazaure I made my first attempts to ride. I had been instructed to bring saddlery from England. The SDO, on leave when I arrived, left a pony for me to buy for £12. So I acquired Buster and became eligible for that mark of the truly Northern officer, horse allowance at £4 a month. Buster was a neat, sturdy, but bad-tempered polo pony whose evil inclinations I never fully mastered. For months I presumed it was my own incompetence. Then one day at a lunch party I overheard his former owner explain why he had sold him: "Always tossing his head and biting, a pity because he was a beautiful turner."

My lack of skill was not helped by an inadequate bit. For a year I rode Buster with a broken snaffle before I realized that only a fool rides a Nigerian stallion with less than a curb. I had often refused offers of the cruel local bit, so my emir's representative, who was elderly and liked a quiet ride, used to order my horseboy to walk in front of me. Since he had found the horseboy his orders were much more effective than mine, and I put up with this indignity until one day when some village youths, knowing both Buster's weakness and mine, pushed a mare out in front of us on a narrow path. The horseboy went flying. I finished an hour and six miles later, to my triumph still seated, and the mare, to Buster's chagrin, unmounted.

From Kazaure I returned to Kano for the weekend. My diary records that at 8 A.M. on Sunday morning I was taken to meet the Emir. Native authorities in Moslem areas kept Friday as a holiday and made a pretense of working on Sundays. A particularly irritating habit of the larger authorities was to hold council meetings which required the presence of the DO early on a Sunday morning. That few, if any, administrative officers ever had the courage to protest is indicative of the strength of the native authorities and the mystique of indirect rule.

The Emir Abdullahi Bayero was an aged and pious man. The day-to-day running of the emirate was largely in the hands of his powerful son, the *Ciroma,* who was to succeed to the throne in 1954. On this occasion I was taken in and introduced, dressed in suit and first carefully inspected by the DO. We shook hands. I mumbled a few words of Hausa and the old man discussed me in the third person with the DO, whose deferential manner I recall to this day. The purpose of the interview over, we were ushered out by the innumerable barefooted and red-and-green-robed *dogarai*[3] and other household attendants. This was to be the only occasion I was to enter the palace, vast and magnificent if somewhat tawdry in the use of twentieth-century decorations. I did, however, meet the Emir on two subsequent occasions when I was in a line-up for handshaking at the Moslem festivals of Id el Fitr and Id el Kabir.

But convention had been satisfied. I could now be sent off into the emirate on my own. First, however, I joined a cadet, a year my senior, to learn the touring routine. An ADO in headquarters told me I was having it soft. "If the SDO had been here, you would have gone off from the station on arrival." I was told the story of the cadet who had been unwise enough to arrive the previous year with a wife, and worse still, two children. When sent on tour he inquired about his family, because cadets in Kano were not given houses. "Buy a horse for your wife and donkey for your children," was the reply.

I left Kano by local train. With me were my touring team, a feature of Kano Division. There was a burly ex-serviceman government messanger, by name Adamu Banana and not really a Nigerian at all for he hailed from French territory. His main task seemed to be the inspection of the quarters prepared for me each day. Government messengers were considered best qualified to comment on the curious sanitary arrangements Europeans demanded, and Adamu, and others after him, invariably had altera-

3. The personal bodyguards and messengers of emirs.

tions made to what seemed to me pretty well perfect privacy and cleanliness. Of equal status in practice, but higher in theory, was the emir's representative. The policy of indirect rule demanded that all I said be conveyed to district heads through this official. In practice he merely sat in on everything and acted as a reporter to the *Ciroma's*[4] office. Provided I didn't humbug him and the district heads gave him suitable presents he caused no problems and I recall him with affection and respect. Two *dogarai* made up the team. One, old enough to be my grandfather, rode on ahead to give warning of my approach, prepare lodgings, and generally hustle the village. I seldom saw him. The other was young and unmounted. He traveled with the carriers, wielding an alarming whip. In fact he was shy and nervous, and spoke with a stammer.

All of this team were in a way beyond the law. They could throw their weight about unchecked, as could my servants. They seemed moderate to me, and no doubt were, but I was conscious that not only did I not know what really transpired but could have done little about it even if I had. They could make life easy or difficult for the cadet in their care. In some respects they soon got the upper hand. My seniors often spoke with nostalgia of the advantages of trekking by night. My first hot season I resolved to try. When I announced my intentions it was obvious that neither messenger nor emir's representative was happy. In true Northern fashion they politely concurred but failed to co-operate. They deceived me about the distance of the journey and arranged for my loads to get lost. Setting off at two in the light of a full moon and after a good sleep I reveled in the ride. In theory I should have arrived about eight and found bath and breakfast waiting, for the carriers had left immediately after I had dined the evening before. My destination was not sighted until noon and bath and breakfast appeared over the horizon two hours later. There was mock anger at the *dogari* who, stammering worse than ever, won my compassion. Thereafter we trekked by day, however great the heat.

4. The *Ciroma* was the senior NA official ranking next to the Emir. He **was** responsible for the districts.

Servants were just the same. I gave in to Buba very early on. To insure a balanced diet and to enjoy to the full the pleasures of aristocratic living I ordered my meals in advance each day. Buba found this irksome and preferred to give me what suited him. He bided his time until one very wet day in August. I had ridden all day, leaving at dawn after a hasty breakfast, to carry out an inquiry in a distant village while my camp moved on an easy five miles. I got in about five soaked through, tired, and very hungry. I called for lunch. With the blandest of smiles Buba said there was no lunch, I had forgotten to order the menu before leaving! He won. From that day on I never once ordered a meal or questioned what I ate. By and large I fed well and was spared much trouble.

For a week I trekked in southern Kano with my host. Self-contained in our households, we did not share lodgings, and care was taken to see that the senior had the better. We solemnly dined with one another on alternate nights. I was suffering from initial loneliness and looked forward to these evenings in company, but a year on his own in bush had already given my colleague the need for quiet and privacy which I was soon to acquire and which is the mark of many Englishmen in Africa. He was a man of high intellect and one of many postwar recruits who found the frustrations too restricting and left after his probationary three years to shine elsewhere. I learned from him of the difficulties facing junior touring officers. He showed me the Kano touring instructions. "District heads should be given a mat to sit on." The first district head we met, a son of the Emir, had a Buick saloon, a Chevrolet pickup, and a motorcycle for visiting his farms. His office was equipped with seats from a crashed wartime transport plane, an assortment of chiming clocks, and that most desirable of all objects in the bush, a kerosene refrigerator. Needless to say we gave him a chair when he called at the resthouse.

"Shake hands only with the district head and not with him in the presence of the emir." "All visitors should remove their shoes when calling on you." The majority followed these time-honored customs without thought, but the younger and better educated native authority officials were searching for contact and beginning to question the validity of behavior which applied to one society and not to another. Many of us were sensitive enough to modify the rules so that we caused no offense. As time went on I began to go out of my way to force social development. It seemed false to push political development and yet remain so nervous of undermining traditional authority. My impression was that generally the older generation accepted that the younger could legitimately behave differently. It was all part of the new-fangled education. Handshaking caused fewer problems than shoe-removing, which until the coup of January 15, 1966, remained a dangerously controversial issue in Northern Nigeria. I once watched a couple of NA clerks argue for five minutes before entering my resthouse whether or not to remove their shoes. They knew perfectly well that a Southern clerk in my office could walk in with his shoes on without question. Were they not all Nigerians? A useful device in the early days was to kick off my own shoes as visitors arrived. The shy man felt less worried and the aggressive received a check.

Umpiring at the middle school sports with Maitama Sule, later to become the most socially radical of the Northern ministers in Lagos, I argued that all societies had customs and removing shoes was merely a mark of good manners and respect. It didn't really matter. Maitama, however, expressed the resentment of the younger generation at what he felt to be degrading. "When the Emir comes to give away the prizes," he said, "everyone here will pull off his shoes and bow down in respect, except you Europeans and the Southerners. Why should I show my inferiority while you display your superiority?"

Apart from instructions out of keeping with the changing times, Kano cadets were hard hit by lack of transport other than horse or cycle. For much of our work these were ideal, but often they geared us down to a pace that aggravated other frustrations. Touring areas might be three days' trek from Kano, and carriers were all but impossible to find at the official rates close to the urban center. The alternative was to hire a native authority pickup. This was wildly unreliable. If a senior NA official wanted the transport he always got priority, and I sometimes wasted two or three days sitting packed up ready to leave before a vehicle finally materialized. Most irksome of all was to arrive at a district boundary to be met by a district head in a large American car. One could not courteously refuse his offer of a lift, which whisked one rapidly to a resthouse where one could do nothing but sit on the floor yearning for bath and drink for two to four hours while the carriers caught up. One could not easily begin the usual tour of inspection. Apart from being dressed for riding and dirty after a trek, there was seldom room to squeeze the emir's representative into the front seat along with driver and praise-singers. For him to have sat in the back with the DH was unthinkable. Moreover, Nigerians regarded traveling as work. They did not expect, at least in the peaceful rural areas, anybody to do other than rest after a journey.

In Kano we hired cycles at 6*d*. an hour from the bicycle-hirer outside the Emir's Nassarawa Palace. I was always struck by the fact that if I was lucky enough to get a lift to the NA offices in the city a *dogari* would rush up to open the door. When I cycled down nobody ever offered to prop up my machine! Some of the district heads were sympathetic and generous in helping out. I often hired a lorry from the jovial *Sarkin Rano* for the price of my carriers, an arrangement I concealed from my masters, who, had they known, would have been less worried by the possibility of corruption of the mind than of the flesh.

*

I was called back to Kano after ten days and sent out on my own to the northeastern touring area. Again I left Kano by train and again encountered the irritating inefficiency which was the hallmark of the railway. Together with the surly stupidity of some of its Southern officials it helped breed the pro-Northern sentiments of so many British officials. It took me two hours of hard work to get myself, staff, and loads onto the local train. It seemed as though I was doing something unprecedented, but for forty years district officers had traveled by train in this way. Argument, long conversations between officials in languages I could not understand, appeals to higher authority, periods when everyone seemed to lose interest altogether, and at last, for no apparent reason, capitulation. In all this my servants and touring team were of no help. W. R. Crocker, writing of a similar experience in the thirties, explained:

As my servants were all Northerners, it was useless sending them: all clerks and subordinate officials in Nigeria, including Northern Nigeria, are Southerners, and in general not only do they not attend to what a Northerner (although the servant of an official) asks of them, but they go out of their way to humiliate him.[5]

I had watched the *furor Africanus* slowly rise in passengers on the ship out and reach boiling point in the Apapa customs shed, and I had resolved never to give way. It was the system rather than the individual which was at fault, and I believed that, given time, I could talk the most hostile into co-operation, and on the whole I succeeded. Most Europeans were automatically rude to Southerners so institutionalized had attitudes become. Naturally the Southerner was at best defensive, but soon warmed to sympathetic treatment. I never could, however, reconcile myself to his usual contempt of the "bush" Northerner.

I was met at Ringim by the *Tafida*, the district head. He was a rival candidate to the Kano succession and therefore disliked by the *Ciroma*. As a consequence the district was neglected and kept short of development funds. The *Tafida* drove me himself in his Buick. This was as unusual for a Kano aristocrat as it must have been for an eighteenth-century English gentleman to have driven his own carriage. Within half an hour of arrival at the resthouse I had my first taste of Nigerian politics. Ringim, an important groundnut-buying center, had a substantial trading and laboring class as well as peasant farmers. The Northern Elements Progressive Union, the Hausa opposition party to the establishment, already had adherents. Two young men came and spilled out a long tale of complaint. My Hausa was insufficient for me to understand much, and both emir's representative and messenger were settling into their lodgings. Indeed the complainants had not appeared until they were safely out of the way. Believing

5. *Nigeria: Critique of British Colonial Administration* (London: Allen and Unwin, 1936), p. 97.

in the efficacy of letting off steam, I encouraged them with suitable noises—Hausa luckily lending itself more than most languages to this happy device. After an hour they began to wind up and I summoned enough Hausa to tell them to return on the morrow, which they did. Then, following the correct procedures, I listened again with the *Tafida* and the emir's representative. I allowed the *Tafida* to take what seemed sensible action without comment. As so often in Nigeria it was the airing of complaint to authority that gave satisfaction rather than the rectification of wrong.

Politics was new to the North and British officials were apprehensive. Suspicions grew with each irresponsible nationalist speech and apparent attack on traditional authority. I am sure we were much too thin-skinned, and our sensitivity helped create the character of political parties which was to grow more sordid until their overthrow in 1966. The complaints the Ringim NEPU put before me were reasonable and legitimate. They spoke on behalf of everyone including the *Tafida*—the district was deliberately neglected as part of an emiral power struggle. NEPU gave an organizational umbrella and courage to a few of the younger men to speak out what were the sentiments of all, and it was their speaking out at all which shocked their elders, not what they said. All my dealings with NEPU in the early days were of this kind. I believe that if we had only refused to be shocked, as were the elders, that some form of public opinion was emerging because of the development we had initiated, NEPU might have become the moderate reformist party which the country was soon to need. In Mallam Aminu Kano it seemed to have a leader of intelligence and moderation who was also well liked by a great many of the better educated. Instead it sank lower and lower until it was the focal point of every town ruffian and village bully. Brute force overpowered the better elements and the latter earned opprobrium which they did not deserve. Bicycle-hirers, for example, were usually NEPU supporters. I knew many and I always found them honest businessmen, clean and smart in appearance, as well as progressive in thought. They had moved right out of a subsistence economy into the world of money. They liked to feel coin in their pockets all the year through and not just at harvest time. For the most part without any formal education, their eyes and ears were wide open to the sights and sounds of the Western world. They had rejected the traditional way of life and with it some of the traditional restraints. Properly handled they could have been a powerful ally in modernization—but most British officials accepted their wholesale condemnation by traditional authorities as ne'er-do-wells. The stability which traditional authority had given the country seemed too precious to jeopardize by needless experiments in political progress to satisfy a vocal and restless minority.

❀

For two days I looked around the various institutions in Ringim: the school, the dispensary, the market; I sat in the court while cases were tried; I talked to the district officials—the sanitary inspector, the forest guard, and the veterinary assistant; I checked the books and counted the cash. Then I set off to visit other villages on my way to Jahun, another district. It was September and those dewy early mornings in which I rode through the sandy scrub, among perhaps twenty heavily robed and besworded horsemen, made me feel like a medieval knight. It was just as well that I felt good, because I doubt if I did much good. My advice, I was soon to discover, fell upon deaf ears both above and below. But maybe my very presence helped. Villagers received a reminder, however infrequent, that law and order existed beyond the immediate horizon, that there were other authorities than their district and village heads; and villages often received a much needed spring-cleaning. For the inquisitive it was also an opportunity to learn what was afoot in the outside world. Unlike the NA officials the Englishman held meetings and talked. I carried, in hesitant and ungrammatical Hausa, news of constitutional change. There was little understanding, but it was a beginning.

The daily routine was to rise with the predawn call to prayer, never missed as, more often than not, I was lodged in the imam's compound. I believed in breakfast and drank a lot of coffee. I never carried water with me by day, and indeed had nothing in which to carry it. My ability to ride all day without drink—and more extraordinary, without urinating—was to mark me out and earn me a nickname. Buba miraculously cooked breakfast and packed at the same time. As I emerged he collapsed table and chair, and the carriers who had long been sitting around seized their loads with much merriment and chafing. There were popular and unpopular loads and always a butt who was left with the worst—not necessarily the heaviest as shape seemed to matter more, although I tried to standardize with wooden beer cases as containers.

Greetings all round, into the saddle, and away in the soft morning light at the special half-walk half-trot common to Hausa horsemen. The village head and his retainers accompanied me through his terrain. At the boundary the next group, waiting since dawn for fear of being late, galloped forward. Farewells and welcomes and off again, stopping in important villages and inspecting anything inspectable. Kano districts, except a few favored ones, had little to show outside district headquarters other than cement-lined wells. Well-sinking, unspectacular and unsung, probably made more difference to the pattern of life in the northern emirates in the forties and fifties than any other factor.

We rode single file along the bush paths. Sometimes I sat and daydreamed, at others I fired questions over my shoulder about the countryside, the crops, the trees, the plants, the animals, and the birds. Usually by noon I arrived at the village which was to be home for a night. By 1951 the great network of resthouses built and used by the early administration had largely fallen into disrepair. Shortage of staff during the war reduced touring, and it never again assumed the same magnitude. Law and order had long since been established, there was much more headquarters office work, and senior officers were using cars. So most nights I stayed in a compound in a village. The large entrance hut, called *zaure* in Hausa, was cleaned and swept and sprinkled with fresh sand. Grass matting porches were built front and back to make three rooms, shield me from the public gaze, and cut me off from the compound of which I formed a part. These lodgings were always delightful, and Buba soon had them organized and comfortable, table and chair in the front, bed and loads in the center, bath and washbasin in the back. Lunch, a read, or perhaps a sleep, were followed about five by a stroll through the village and a meeting with the elders. For this some form of rickety and dirty chair was always produced. I much preferred the mortar for corn-grinding hastily upturned as I went through villages by day. Hausa society had in those days little use for furniture. The wealthiest were content to sit as had their forefathers on a mat.

Meetings followed a pattern. I slowly built up to the real business, thus allowing everyone to get used to my voice and, indeed, realize that I was speaking an apology for their language. I began with formal greetings and polite inquiries about health and crops and needs. In Kano the answers were always the same. Everything was perfect, nothing was wanted, and everyone was delighted to see me. After these preliminaries I spoke of the current issue, in those early days pending constitutional change and the electoral procedures in which all would soon take part. Finally I added suitable homilies for the particular village, perhaps about guinea worm, or groundnut fertilizer, or late planting of cotton. The elders, white-haired and bearded, sat crouched on the ground, heads leaning over in respectful silence to the nonsense talked by the boy young enough to be their grandchild. Messenger, or emir's representative, or sometimes district head, repeated sentence by sentence what I said. The officious type of village head frequently interpolated a "You've heard what the white man says?" to which all dutifully replied in an affirmative chorus.

Village meeting over in time for prayers, I sometimes walked out into the surrounding farms. But Kano was fearful of officers who stretched their legs alone, and I never got used to the company of the *dogari* sent to insure that I neither caused trouble nor got lost. He would disturb the evening peace by shouting to late workers or homecomers to run forward to greet me on bended knee. If I spoke to a passer-by he had to act as intermediary. On our return he would report to the emir's representative. Those around me felt responsible. They feared great trouble for themselves should I do anything foolish. They therefore kept close watch. From resthouses, sited away from villages, I did however often escape unobserved, and as time went on my desire to climb any hill in sight was accepted as a foolish eccentricity, although I knew that nobody felt fully at ease until I was reported safely back.

I would sit on some hilltop looking down on the village where I was staying, watch the blue smoke of cooking fires rising through the thatched roofs, and listen to the quiet, reassuring sounds of village life: the peculiar thump, thump of pestle in mortar, the crow of a rooster, small boys' calling to one another as they energetically pursued a wayward goat, and the polite murmur of greetings as compound heads returned home. I would reflect upon not only the orderliness of the farms around me, but the ordered society of which they were the product. The simplicity, peace, and sense of continuity of prosperous Hausa village life was something to admire. It seemed so unnecessary to disrupt it for the sake of progress, yet the Hausa peasant could not avoid contact with the century in which he lived and whose aircraft already droned overhead. Introducing change without destroying stability, bringing new values but retaining the old, was to be the essence of my job.

At dusk I bathed and changed, not into the evening dress of the cartoonist's imagination, but into slacks, long-sleeved shirt, and mosquito boots. The latter became a habit I have never shed. Worn without socks, a useful economy, they are cool and comfortable as well as protective. My pressure lamp would provide street lighting such as villages seldom saw. It was a magnet to children as well as insects. I always sat outside and had a drink in the still night air. I would hear the twitterings of small bodies jostling for a better view. This was the time to set up the gramophone. The carriers, used to me and friendly with my servants, showed their special relationship by coming closer and settling down around my chair to listen. Soon the braver of the village children and youths would join them, until I sometimes had an audience of several hundred. Their favorites were Hausa praise songs and a record called "The Laughing Policeman." Night after night I listened to the same virtues of the great and the raucous laughter of the policeman. Both jarred on my ears, but my heart filled with pleasure at the reaction of the audience. Only at these moments did I ever feel any communion with the people whom I was supposed to serve. We never conversed and they went away silently afterward. But they had received some little recompense for the hustling and bustling my visit caused. Evenings sitting out under the stars and with a rising moon have delighted most expatriates in Northern Nigeria. Mine were even richer and I can never think of them without great nostalgia.

I had been given no specific jobs on my first tour. I stayed out four weeks, tasting what Hastings called "the soul of life out there. It [trekking] makes for health and hardening, it gives us constant change of scene which is refreshing, and adds each day to our experience. More than that, it is the essence of our work in Nigeria."[6] At the beginning of September I submitted my first report.[7]

I arrived back in Kano in mid-October feeling very pleased with myself. I was enjoying my work and daily gaining confidence. I had lots of questions to ask and my head was buzzing with ideas for the improvement of Ringim and Jahun Districts. I had liked both district heads and felt that I had made a reasonable impression. The substantive Senior District Officer was back from leave. I reported on arrival. Entry to his office was regulated by an elderly messenger who no longer felt it necessary, in his exalted place and close to retirement, to defer to junior officers. He mumbled greetings from his seat and pointed through the open window at the piles of files behind which the SDO worked. I hung about half an hour or so until Fada decided that the time was opportune for me to enter. I introduced myself as one of the new cadets and explained that I had just come in from tour.

"Ah, yes. I have just been reading your touring report." I felt ten feet tall, and waited for questions, perhaps even commendation.

"Have you got a typewriter?"

6. Hastings, *Nigerian Days*, p. 153.
7. See p. 120 below.

"Yes, Sir."

"Always type everything in triplicate. It's a great help. You must come and have a drink sometime."

Thus dismissed I felt like catching the next plane home. The Northern Nigerian service was a curious mixture of comradeship, hospitality, often immense kindness, and of public school brutality and pettiness. H. B. Hermon Hodge, writing of his first arrival in Lokoja in 1908, said, "Not a soul met me, nobody knew anything about me, nor did anyone apparently care."[8] This tradition survived. The SDO had no doubt had the Hermon Hodge treatment in his early days. It probably did not occur to him that there might be better and happier methods. I never did feel at ease with the SDO thereafter, indeed I avoided him. The Senior Resident was even more remote, for not only had he the unique advantage of a second resident to assist in running the province, but he was also much involved in business at Kaduna, the headquarters of the Northern Provinces. I solemnly signed his visitors' book every time I came in from bush to indicate my presence, but I did not meet him for five months and then only by chance. Later in my career I was to know him well, however, and to respect him greatly. The rest of the administration were very friendly, but I was left with a sense of being not only unimportant but useless. It had the effect (perhaps intended) of sending me back to bush immediately.

Before I left I was asked by the DO in charge of development to make a number of road reconnaissances and also instructed to conduct a pilot census in a village of my own choosing in preparation for the national census due the next year. These special duties added interest and gave a purpose around which to plan the trek. At the end of each month I submitted a touring report and the special reports as I finished the assignments.[9]

I never saw anybody else's reports and nobody commented upon mine. It was not until I had to draft for a senior man that I received any tuition. The verbiage of early reports I put down to

8. *Up against It in Nigeria* (London: Allen and Unwin, 1922), p. 17.
9. See pp. 126 and 135 below.

the slow pace of work. Writing a report, composing on the typewriter, was a way to pass a morning and a relief from trying to be busy among people whose staying power seldom exceeded a couple of hours. My use of the passive was due to a belief that civil service writing must always be cloaked in anonymity. Although I was picking things up fast, I still had little idea of how to get any follow-up to proposals I made. I also seldom knew just how much or how little knowledge my masters had about my touring area. I really had immense freedom but would have profited from closer supervision.

After I had been around my districts for the second time I began to look beyond the routine. I enjoyed the various inspections, particularly those of schools, but wanted to do something more positive. I would sometimes spend a whole morning in a school concentrating on some particular aspect, spoken English preferably, but few Kano primary schools taught English in 1951. There seemed so much to do and yet little means of accomplishing anything.

So the new district council in Jahun seemed to be an exciting prospect. I had come too late to have much to do with its establishment but, finding time on my hands, satisfied my creative instincts by proposing a training scheme for the recently elected councilors.[10] I didn't really expect anything to come out of my suggestion although I kept it as simple as possible in the hope that I would be told to go ahead. A little later in my career I would have gone ahead and said nothing about it, but at the time I presumed that the district head would want orders from Kano before he could take part, in which presumption I was probably correct. I also wanted to show my superiors that I could do more than ride along road lines and chase cattle. The past might be fun but the future was knocking at the door.

I suggested three days spent by all the councilors in the district headquarters to improve their knowledge of what developments

10. See p. 139 below.

were taking place in agriculture and hygiene. These seemed not only the most important aspects of life for a rural community but were the only ones in which anything worthwhile could be organized at district level. Soil conservation and mixed farming were the agricultural points I wanted to put across. The hygiene sessions were to tackle common local ailments, particularly guinea worm, and demonstrate some of the protective methods already adopted in Kano urban area for the sale of cooked foodstuffs. It was all very simple, and I regret that I never had the go-ahead to implement my scheme. In a few years this kind of course was to be a feature of the Institute of Administration at Zaria and councilors were only too ready to learn something of model local government practice as well as improve their usefulness to the community by gaining knowledge of a wide variety of skills common in other societies but lacking in their own. Nobody in the average village, for example, would know how to nail on a pan roof, fix a door hinge, or mix cement. The wise expenditure of district council funds often depended on supervision by a councilor who had learned about modern buildings at the institute.

When all else failed to keep me busy I would pass my time in the local court. In Kano each district had a court in which an *alkali*, a Moslem judge, tried both civil and criminal cases according to Islamic law. It has become popular to criticize these courts and to compare them unfavorably with magistrates' courts. The assumption was that the *alkali* would be in the pocket of the native authority, his employer, and the district head who represented the NA on the spot. In practice he very rarely was, and personally I would much have preferred trial before an honest *alkali* than an expatriate magistrate, who relied very heavily on bad and often corrupt interpreters, and argued rules of court the average Nigerian could not possibly understand with lawyers often as ignorant as himself of the cultural background of the accused.

The *alkali* courts might have been a trifle careless over matters of record, but justice was clearly seen to be done and the large number of civil cases, some brought by Christian Southerners, heard each month in any Kano district was in itself evidence that the public was reasonably satisfied with the system. The *alkalai* themselves had a special status which clearly indicated their independence of the district head. They were subject to the chief alkali in Kano and not to the councilor responsible for district administration. I noticed, for example, that the *alkali* would come to greet me on arrival in a district with formality and of his own accord, whereas other employees would be lined up by the district head. When I visited the court the district head would always send to inquire if it was convenient, whereas he would walk into any other institution unheralded.

There were, of course, bad *alkalai*, but there were bad magistrates too in whose courts unscrupulous lawyers had a free hand while the ignorant peasant was protected from them in the so-called native courts. Islamic law, of course, with its emphasis on the oath leaves little room for counsel's argument, and although perjury became commonplace as politics spread, it was a rarity in 1951 in the districts.

A district officer had the right to review cases, but I never did this if an avenue of appeal existed, except to adjust technical errors by a court such as exceeding its powers of jurisdiction or punishment, and then I would review the case on my own motion. Sitting in court was not only a check on possible abuses, the worst of which was usually delay, but gave one a picture of the society in which one worked. Theft was the commonest criminal case, and theft of farm crops likeliest to draw forth the heaviest sentences, understandable in a peasant farming community. Divorce was the commonest civil matter, and I quickly discarded some of my preconceived prejudices about Islamic treatment of women when I saw the ease with which a woman could bring a complaint against her husband. I was also impressed by the patience and skill of many an *alkali* in trying first to reconcile quarreling couples.

Needless to say a day in court was very good for my Hausa. The proceedings over, I would often borrow the court record book so that I could at leisure work out what had not been clear to me at the time. Many Kano court records were, however, still kept in *ajami* at this time—that is, Hausa written in Arabic rather than Roman script—and this I never mastered.

✿

As well as sending in monthly reports we made entries in the District Note Books. These were a wonderful collection of comments over the years on projects and personalities. They reflected the current fashions in administration, one man perhaps painstakingly recording the genealogy of every village head, another entering market prices, and so on. Some officers regarded the books as a waste of time, and this was an especially common view among those who had taken to motorcar touring. The note books were bulky to carry, and, of course, if you did not make the entries while in the district there was little chance that it would be done once you were back in the office. To those who trekked, however, and especially to newcomers, the note books provided not only useful information about the districts but about predecessors, and were a pleasant diversion in the long and lonely days in bush. I had read Crocker[11] while at Oxford and since arrival in Kano felt the truth of many of his criticisms. But his comments in District Note Books lessened my sympathy. His resthouses were always the most bat and snake infested, the rains were wetter and the harmattan dustier wherever he trekked. Perhaps he really had been the difficult young man his seniors thought as they rapidly posted him from one province to another.

I indulged in what I thought was fair comment in the note books. They were confidential and frankness seemed no fault. But after my first return to Kano and encounter with the SDO, I—as Crocker must have done—worked out personal frustrations in the note book of Gabasawa District. Not only was I feeling miserable but, compared to Ringim and Jahun, the district was miserable. The DH was an oily type who cringed away and refused to shake my hand, something I had not come across before and found

11. W. R. Crocker was an administrative officer in the thirties. His *Nigeria: Critique of British Colonial Administration* was the only critical analysis generally available when I was a cadet.

distasteful. He treated me with suspicion. I was soon convinced that either the last ADO to visit or the DH was a bad man. I knew the ADO was not. The forestry assistant was elegantly dressed, and obviously useless, never setting foot outside the town. The scribe was equally elegant and drenched in scent. Despite his appearance and simpering mannerisms he proved a sturdy trekker and sensible adviser on the road survey. The prison was full of men awaiting trial and no effort was being made to hear the cases. I commented vigorously and facetiously. Soon afterward the Resident visited the district. It was typical of Kano and the attitudes which built up the resentments I had worked out that I, supposedly in charge of the touring area, was not required in person. (The same month I found another ADO on tour in Jahun hunting *jangali*.[12] Normally tied to an office schedule and wanting a few days break in bush, he had asked where he could help out on *jangali* and was allowed to go to Jahun, nobody either telling him that I was there, or me that he was coming. The DH was embarrassed not knowing with whom to travel. It was hard to keep up prestige in these circumstances, harder still morale.)

When I returned to Kano I still felt hurt that the Resident had preferred the District Note Book to me. I now found my first rocket awaiting in the form of a minute to the DO:

Some of the comments made by Mr. Smith in the Gabasawa District Note Book are in very bad taste and should be expunged. The worst are under the following heads:
DH: "I feel instinctively that he is a cad"
Forestry: "apart from looking chic . . ."
District scribe: "is not a pansy"
Mr. Smith must learn that these note books, which are valuable official records are not to be used for puerile displays of "cleverness." There is no objection whatever to criticism of NA staff provided that it is couched in moderate terms and based on something more valuable than "instinct," but comments such as those mentioned above are quite

---

12. *Jangali* is the cattle tax charged on each head of cattle. Nomadic herdsmen pay no other direct taxes. It was a tradition of the service that young officers played at cowboys once a year and went searching for missing herds. It was very much a game, relieved the tedium of routine touring, and sometimes increased revenue.

valueless and most unsuitable. In his comment on the prison the words "DH and *alkali* told to get cracking" suggest that Mr. Smith does not yet fully understand his position vis a vis the NA.

In future I should like to see the touring diaries or touring notes of all ADOs each time they come into Kano.

I deserved the rocket, and the Resident kindly had me up for a drink to soften the blow, and perhaps, as the third paragraph of his minute suggests, because he felt a trifle guilty about his ignorance of what we were all up to. Suitably chastened I set off to bush once more, this time with an instruction to investigate population movement within the province. Settlement schemes were a current fad and a way to make a reputation. My assignment was a preliminary to a possible scheme. I set off with little to go on, no knowledge of demography, and no idea how to proceed. But it sounded interesting and I welcomed a special assignment as opposed to general touring. A month later I submitted my report.[13]

It was based on interviews with village and hamlet heads and a study of the annual tax census conducted in every village area. I had begun something which was to grow and grow over the years and keep me busy off and on for several months. I began in Ungogo and Kumbotso Districts close to Kano itself to see just how far land pressure was driving farmers away from the densely populated and intensively cultivated environs of the city to seek new land elsewhere. I then visited two districts in the southern part of the province, Kiru and Karaye, to see how far anyone had been moving in to farm and from where they came. As always when we visited districts on special assignments I carried out the usual inspections. The two small districts close to Kano were not included in any touring area and seldom visited except on evening drives by the SDO. Kiru and Karaye were in the southern touring area from which the ADO had recently gone on leave and not been replaced, so that I felt free to carry on where he had left off. My visits to these districts coincided with the annual announcement of tax. This was an exciting occasion and in Kano Emirate an event of some importance and value, for every village

13. See p. 144 below.

and hamlet head, as well as a substantial number of elders, were gathered together in the district headquarters for several days.

The general (or income) tax was assessed at a rate per tax-payer (adult males) by the native authority and approved by the government. An annual tax census was conducted before the preparation of the budget. Within the framework of the tax rate, assessments could vary from district to district, village to village, and taxpayer to taxpayer. It was the duty of the village head, with the advice of his elders, to assess individuals according to their circumstances. In practice this meant that a few wealthy men paid a little more than the rate and the old, infirm, and first-year payers paid rather less. A boy was usually included on the list once he began to farm on his own account, which might be within a year or two of puberty.

An administrative officer, usually accompanied by a senior NA official, announced the rate to the assembled crowd, often a thousand or more strong, and handed over to each hamlet head in turn a note recording the total tax due from his hamlet. There was plenty of good-natured chafing as the amounts were called out. I would make a speech in which I tried to explain that tax paid was used for services rendered, but with so little to see physically in return, it was hard to make an impression on the widely held belief that tax was a tribute and went into the pockets of those collecting it—some turning up for King George, whose head appeared on the shillings used in payment. The majority of NA officials tended to foster this view in their own interests. Anything provided for a district thus became a gift from the emir through the intermediary of a local traditional ruler. I often wondered how much of the tax villagers thought I acquired, although there was little logic in their reasoning as it was also widely believed that Europeans could go to their friends, the bankers, and obtain as much money as they required.

At the end of tax announcement there was the inevitable exhortation from the district head to be prompt in payment. With pockets full from the groundnut crop, Kano tax was often collected within a matter of days, and with an efficiency that might have been the envy of many more sophisticated tax authorities.

Payment was almost entirely in shillings. Paper money was unpopular in rural areas. It was hard to change and vulnerable to the fires that swept through villages during the harmattan. Counterfeit coins were rare, but carefully guarded against. Worn or damaged coins were unacceptable to most people as were shillings dating from a previous reign. Europeans were known to be casual about coinage, and shop assistants and traders passed off their unwanted coins on us. I once paid a carrier with a George V shilling. "This king is dead," he indignantly pointed out, rejecting the coin.

*

December, 1951, was dominated by the later stages of the indirect elections leading to the first majority-elected representative legislature in Nigeria. Compared to subsequent elections the procedures were simple and informal. In some ways public opinion was more truly represented than in later elections which tended to subordinate the outcome to bitter dissession over the method. The village primaries were informal gatherings at which we asked potential candidates to stand up and then told supporters to line up behind. For a matter-of-fact and illiterate peasantry, who could not understand what all the fuss was about anyway, this was an acceptable procedure.[14] The election was criticized on the grounds that it produced so many natural rulers as elected representatives. It was presumed that many villagers were afraid to vote for anyone else. From my personal observation this was not the case. There were villages with alternative candidates, and they sometimes won. But where the village head

14. The Kano Annual Report for 1951 began: "It will be a long time before the people of Kano Province forget the year 1951. In Kano City and its immediate environs it will be remembered principally as the year of the El Dunia tragedy when 331 Africans, many of them youths, lost their lives in a terrible cinema fire. To the small minority that understands the purpose and significance of constitutional reform, the outstanding event has been the establishment in an area where government by popular representation was until recently unknown, of an electoral system rooted in every village and based in its later stages on the secret ballot. But to the vast majority of the population to whom party politics and parliamentary processes as yet have little meaning the main feature of 1951 is that after two seasons of anxiety and tightened belts there has been a bumper harvest, said by many to be the best for a decade, and that both their corn bins and their pockets are full again."

was reasonably popular and young enough to travel the natural reaction was to send him off to represent the community—this, after all, was why he was village head. He was expected to suffer the inconveniences which in those early days democracy seemed to imply. NEPU, the opposition party, thrived where there was a bad village head and in bigger towns whose size prevented the rural pattern of intimate communication between ruled and ruler. It had little chance of success in a community with a just and progressive village head, and a great many were both. Many, though not all, village headships were in the gift of the community in the first place. The method of election adopted for the primaries was already familiar as the method of selecting a village head. Candidates for a village headship were usually confined to certain "royal" families but could be many in number in a polygamous society, and confirmation of appointment by district head or emir was virtually automatic after selection by the village community. The advent of regional politics introduced interference with these traditional procedures, with their built-in checks and balances, rather than the reverse.

From the village primaries we moved to the district electoral colleges. I presided over five of these in eight days, traveling furiously to keep up with the timetable. Each election followed the same pattern. I called a roll to make sure that those elected at the primaries and entitled to be present were there and nobody else. I then spent some time explaining the new constitution, what election at the district level would mean, and the procedure to be followed. Radios and newspapers were unknown in the rural areas, the majority illiterate, and horizons narrow. I was surprised at how much understanding existed. The district colleges inevitably contained a majority of village heads, and the district head was invariably nominated as one of the candidates. Again it seemed the natural thing to do. At Kura there were a couple of clean, simply dressed youths who had succeeded in the primaries on behalf of NEPU. They made an interesting contrast to the older of the turbanned village heads who sank to the ground in a flurry of soiled linen every time one looked at them. Some NEPU supporters managed to reach the provincial electoral college. Many of these keen and anxious young men drifted after a few years into the left wing of the NPC.

Voting at the district level was by means of the "whispered ballot." Members of the college came into the polling room one by one and whispered to the returning officer (myself) their choice of candidates. To avoid embarrassment to the literate I made out ballot papers, and those who wished were able to vote in secrecy. The reaction of the district heads was interesting. *Dan Kade,* a former schoolmaster who delighted in correcting my Hausa, was very secretive. The elderly *Wambai* found it ridiculous that I should waste his time and mine asking him. Of course he was voting for himself. The sly *Turaki* inquired first whether he could.

I rushed to Kano with the results and was told to stand by and help with the provincial electoral college due to meet on Monday, December 17, presided over by the Senior Resident. On the Sunday I spent from 10:30 A.M. to 5 P.M. making various arrangements and yearning for a car. On the day itself I was on duty from 7 A.M. until 10:30 P.M. My diary contains the interesting entry: "Shook hands with the Senior Resident!" Together with another cadet whom he had never met I was hastily pushed in front of him at the start of the day's proceedings. My particular job was to record nominations for the twenty seats and get the ballot paper printed. At the NA press I had already arranged for the names of all the college to be set up in both roman and arabic type. Traditional titles as well as names were used, and the final paper with fifty-one candidates measured 24 by 18 inches.

I had been told to be helpful to Inuwa Wada, then a clerk in the electricity department but soon to become a man of great wealth and power, who was an official of the hazily organized NPC, the party allied to traditional authority with the tacit support of the British administration. I advised him that the whispered ballot for illiterates, and even marking a ballot paper by literates, in an election with twenty seats to fill might be confusing. His party would be helped if its candidates were nominated in a block and could thus appear one after another on the ballot paper. (The British tradition of not identifying candidates on a ballot paper except by name was followed in 1951, and sensibly abandoned later.) I did not tell him that if the NPC followed my advice the NEPU candidates would also get nominated in a block. I was uneasy about the instructions I had received and was glad to be able to salve my conscience.

In addition to those who reached the college through the village primaries and district college, native authorities were permitted to inject 20 per cent of their own nominees. This device was a second thought. Most of the educated and administratively experienced men in the North were NA employees, usually working in the central offices. To stand in city primaries was often courting disaster, for not only was NEPU strongest in the towns but there might be the competition of a popular ward head. It looked as though the North could finish up represented at Lagos almost entirely by illiterate and elderly village and district heads. The Kano injection was of the type expected and many were among the twenty who finally won. M. G. Smith has recorded how in Zaria the Emir had already decided who was to be elected.[15] Membership of Parliament became a new form of patronage in all the emirates. So when we began in the morning most of those present knew exactly what the outcome was to be, but for hour upon hour we solemnly went through the rituals of democratic procedure. Just as at the lower levels there was a natural tendency to vote for traditional authorities, so at the highest it seemed natural that the emir in person should be involved in the selection process. The only consolation I derived on the day was that the mighty of Kano had to sit in discomfort on hard wooden chairs, cheek by jowl, hour after hour, without the support of their usual retainers.

✻

After the election came Christmas and then I resumed my usual touring once more. My report on population movement had kept alive the interest in a settlement scheme. I was told to visit a scheme at Daudawa in Katsina Province and then look deeper

15. *Government in Zazzau, 1800–1950* (London: Oxford University Press, 1960), p. 292.

into the prospects for a scheme in Kiru District.[16] To facilitate this I was told to leave the northeastern touring area and take over the southern. I put up proposals for a settlement scheme as well as carrying out the routine touring tasks. I was much too inexperienced to understand how many years might pass before any plan reached the maturity of execution. A few months later I headed a team to investigate the area in greater detail. It was the first time that I had been in bush with professional staff. I was nervous for I was the youngest and least experienced but, by virtue of being an administrative officer, leader of the group. I decided that to fly the usual Union Jack would add insult to injury. On the morning of our departure back to Kano the well-driller, a notorious but delightful character well into his fifties, took me aside. In his broad Scots, patting me on the shoulder, he said: "Laddie, in all the provinces I've been the ADO's fly the old country's flag in the bush. It gives you heart and makes you feel at home. You tell those fuckers who boss you in Kano to give you one too." Eventually the Kiru scheme materialized, and after I had left the province a series of ADO's lived there trying to make it work. As with so much of our job, one never saw the first sprouting of the seeds let alone the fruit.

*

The first quarter of 1952 I settled down to touring the southern area. Although I had enjoyed Ringim and Jahun the southern part of the division was less thickly populated and far more attractive physically. It was well wooded and sprinkled with the rocky hills so typical of Northern Nigeria. I became especially fond of Rano District, whose headquarters at Kibiya I used as my base. Rano was by origin one of the founder Hausa states and, although now part of and subject to Kano, preserved a certain independence. The district headship was confined to the Rano families and could not be tampered with by the Emir of Kano. As a result *Sarkin Rano*, the DH, was not only without emiral ambitions but had firm roots in his district. Most of the best district heads I came across in the emirates had a similar background.

16. See p. 150 below.

Their districts were usually the happiest. The others suffered from Fulani aristocrats who used a district as a steppingstone to better things, spending much of their time visiting the emir in attempts to curry favor or intrigue for promotion to a wealthier district or central councilorship. *Sarkin Rano* lived well. He was the only chief who ever sent me up cooked foods in the usual gift on arrival. It was a pleasant change from the inevitable brace of chicken, eggs, rice, and onions. He took a pride in showing me his district and never got tired of visiting schools, of which there was the comparatively large number of three. After one such visit together we decided to organize an interschool football competition. The day of the great match arrived. A pitch prepared for the occasion was about two miles out of town. I walked to the chief's house where his somewhat unreliable Buick awaited. He had heard from my retinue how I had approved of the *Tafida's* driving himself. To my surprise he announced that he would drive and that I should sit beside him. Others crowded into the back seat, and his driver, left out in the scramble, shouted instructions through the window. Hausa has since imported many English words to cope with the motorcar, but then terms common to horse-riding were more usual. Brakes, accelerator, even gears could be adequately if picturesquely described, but no horse ever had a clutch. After ten minutes we had jerked only a few yards down the sandy road. *Sarkin Rano* was undismayed. Announcing that the engine was broken, he imperiously commanded the admiring bystanders to push, and pushed we were the whole way to and from the match.

With *Sarkin Rano* I established village councils and a district council. He was contemptuous of national political advance, knowing of course that anyone like himself would never stand a chance of representing Kano, a privilege confined to the Fulani rather than the Hausa aristocracy. But he was tolerant of representative local government and always happy to listen to his peasantry speak their minds. He often philosophized about his position as a traditional ruler. Once, as we drove together, he told me that he always waved to his *talakawa* no matter how tired he felt, "because they like it." A few years later he was to be the

model student at a district heads course held at the Institute of
Administration, Zaria. Without prompting he seized a shovel and
began to mix cement at a culvert-making demonstration. His
action delighted the English staff but appalled his Fulani colleagues, who speedily reported his undignified behavior to a
minister. Thereafter came the command that on no account were
district heads to bemean themselves on courses. The poorer type
district head, effete with inbreeding and idleness, had mistaken
the point. *Sarkin Rano* was so self-confident in his aristocratic
pride that he could afford an occasional eccentricity without
disturbing the natural order of society. He and I had the best
possible relationship, and together we were able to do a lot for
Rano.

Life as a touring officer was beginning to look up. The DO who
had been in charge of the division when I first arrived was
assigned the job of co-ordinating development in the districts,
thus spreading the very considerable load carried by the SDO.
He read our reports with interest and acted with vigor. Best of all
he often came out for a night to join us and discuss matters. A
village in Rano District called Tarai had for long provoked ad-
verse comment because of its unusually cramped and filthy condition. On January 9 I submitted a special report on the village
asking for funds to subsidize a new layout to which I had managed to get local agreement. In my February report I was able to
announce that work on a new village site had begun, and before I
left the touring area the job was complete.[17] This kind of follow-
up was an enormous boost to morale and I had never been
happier in my work.

An added excitement at this time was a scare about tsetse fly.
The Trypanosomiasis Research Institute had plotted a major
movement of *Glossina morsitans* northward into the Anchau corridor which had been cleared of flies before the war. Somebody in
the Secretariat threw himself heart and soul into the diversion,
and for several months many of us were partially or fully involved
in the organization of a gigantic clearing operation in the path of
the flies. Tsetse require water and shade for flight. By felling all

17. See pp. 156 and 161 below.

trees, particularly along stream beds, it was possible to halt movement into fly-free areas. My task was to recruit and transport labor from the southern districts of Kano into the sparsely populated corner of Zaria Province where clearing was to take place. I made the trip down the long leg of Tudun Wada District to Riruwe several times. This was the loneliest road in the province. The remnant of one village was the only relief from miles of dense bush. It was known as the village of the blind. Every male in the community became blind in adult life from prolonged contact with the *Simulium damnosum* fly. The women, who did not go into the bush to hunt, were less affected but not unscathed. Needless to say it was not a popular place in which to spend a night, although the risk was small.

Recruiting labor in the dry season was not difficult, but work so far away from home and in the bush was unpopular. I tried to recruit fresh labor every two weeks and allow those who wished to return home to do so. This was my first insight into the amazing ability of Nigerians to improvise and exist in conditions most of us would regard as intolerable. They quickly built themselves shelters of grass, and as soon as cash was flowing traders of one sort or another miraculously appeared out of the bush and set up shop. I was often in later years to witness this speedy generation of economic activity which a labor-intensive project sparked off. By the end of the operation, when the laborers had to return to their farms for planting, the camps had the appearance of small towns. The scheme was at least a partial success. For years afterward the Kudaru Hills looked as though some monster barber had given one side of them a haircut.

❀

Riruwe was my first contact with the attractive country of the central plateau and also with the tin mining community.[18] The only expatriates I had come across in the bush, other than government officials, had been American missionaries from the evangelical Christian churches. These varied a great deal, from the Midwesterner who told me he took orders only from the Almighty

18. See p. 164 below.

and had no intention of complying with the provisions of his certificate of occupancy to the delightful and newly arrived young couple who told me how wonderful it must be to be a British civil servant because all my mail would be franked "On His Majesty's Service"! Needless to say such folk neither smoked nor drank, but they hospitably shared their table and one ate well, if largely from cans. The informal and sometimes unduly prolonged grace I found a strain, particularly on the occasion when the master of the house, having thanked the good Lord for many blessings received that day, included my visit among them. But he added the proviso that "Lord, he is the kind of visitor with whom you would wish us to consort." One seldom saw these missionaries out and about. Their mission had strict rules about wearing sun helmets and keeping women and children indoors during the heat of the day. I felt sorry for the children, who seemed such anemic little kids compared to others of their own age.

The miners were a very different breed. They drank hard and often, and I found myself cursing my too ready acceptance of hospitality. The most foolish thing I did was to join a hunting expedition. I had just acquired a shotgun and had borrowed a rifle, for there was plenty of game around Tudun Wada. I looked forward to learning from experienced hunters. A Frenchman who had lived long in Riruwe had some beautiful leopard skins in his house. I later learned that his method was to lure the leopard with a live goat tied in a trap on his veranda and to shoot it through the eye in the morning with a .22. For the hunt he lined us up and we walked through the bush shooting anything that moved. Each man carried a shotgun for birds and was followed by a bearer with a rifle for larger game. A dangerous procedure. I was glad that it met with little success, and thereafter I resolved to hunt alone. Some of the miners were, alas, shooting freely the restricted oribi and klipspringer which were so rare and so beautiful.

One miner had the good fortune of a charming wife. They were civilized and delightful people. I stayed overnight with them on one occasion, and they did much to restore my faith, pointing out that the rough-and-ready young bachelors employed by some companies were by no means typical of the whole community. They fed me well and I remember exchanging a tin of some curious Dutch confection I had bought by mistake for a can of kippers, the only English delicacy I ever yearned for in the bush. I also had lunch with the Frenchman. The meal was worthy of a Paris restaurant and could not pass without comment from somebody who had been living for months on a diet of roast chicken and baked custard. "Ah, it is nothing," I was told. "The cook and steward are in Jos with my wife; the gardener had to manage."

✿

Other assignments interrupted my regular touring of the southern touring area after March, but I retained an interest and as nobody else was available visited whenever possible. In September I went there on tour with a new cadet to show him the ropes just as they had been shown to me a year before. I took the opportunity to organize a lion hunt. Trekking in Rano and Tudun Wada districts I had often been asked if I had heard the lions roar. The first time was during a river crossing. These were exciting interludes in the day's trek, for the Kano rivers were wide and the water flowed fast during the height of the rains. I and my loads were carried over on a flimsy raft made of cornstalks kept afloat on top of huge gourds. Sometimes a bed was used as the raft. The carriers and other humble fry were either given a gourd to swim themselves over, or made to hold on across one while a youth supplied the propulsion with his legs. The horses were swum over, their heads supported by a boy atop a gourd. The youths and boys who were employed by the *sarkin ruwa*, the local chief waterman, were expert at maneuvering on the gourds, moving at high speed and able to keep completely dry even if fully clothed. They were also powerful if unorthodox swimmers. Their master shouted encouragement from the safety of the bank as they demonstrated their prowess in the swirling water. A crossing might take several hours to complete as the raft went back and forth taking only one or two loads at a time. Crossing the Kano River between Rano and Tudun Wada districts I espied *Dan*

Kade, the district head, awaiting me on the opposite bank a quarter of a mile away across the flooded river. I went over first to greet him, and to allow my Rano followers to set off home. When I reached the bank there was an unnatural silence, everyone listening intently. "Did you hear the lion?" No, I had been far too intent on keeping dry as I squatted on the little platform a dozen burly lads were pushing through the torrent.

It was many months before I really believed in the lion, and even then I was never certain that I had heard it roar. But I saw kills. In Rano, lions were blamed for keeping the nomad cattle away, and so I suggested to the newly formed district council that they put a bounty on any lion killed. This they did. By September, kills were becoming more frequent, and encouraged by news of the bounty a group of hunters came north from the game-ridden bush of Tudun Wada. For two days we sat and listened to reports until we were able to plot the location of what I was convinced could only be the one creature. I hoped to take a shot at him myself, but foolishly did not let it be known that I was not interested in the bounty. We planned a dawn hunt. I sent the hunters on ahead the evening before, intending to ride out before dawn to meet them. They left Kibiya beating drums, blowing horns, firing guns, and exploding firecrackers.

They got the lion that very evening. The poor fellow was so disturbed by the racket that he roused himself from his slumbers after a heavy meal of a calf to find a quieter place to rest. When we brought the body in about noon a crowd of thousands had swarmed into Kibiya from all over the district as the news of the kill had spread overnight. There was enormous excitement and the lucky hunter received a larger sum of money than he had ever had in his life before. It was a curious moment. In all that vast crowd gathered in the African bush only the two Englishmen and the head hunter had ever seen a lion before!

Part 2. On Special Duties

The advent of ministerial government at both regional and central levels called for increased administrative staff in headquarters. As recruitment was slowing down the only possible source was the provinces. By mid-1952 Kano was running on fewer staff than for several years. The luxury of two Residents was short-lived, and a number of junior officers were pulled into the newly formed ministries and much enlarged Civil and Financial Secretaries' Offices. To utilize the remaining provincial staff it was decided to change from the traditional allocation of duties by geographical touring areas to a functional system. This experiment was to be repeated time and time again over the next ten years but never proved wholly successful. The demand and, indeed, need for an all-purpose administrative officer on the spot has survived in Northern Nigeria until the present day, despite chronic shortage of staff to meet the growing responsibilities of a governmental machine that continually broadens its field of activities.

It was intended that I should concentrate on local government, which meant the development of district councils. Without transport it was a tall order. To trek from district to district over an area of just under sixteen thousand square miles with only one objective would have been a ridiculous waste of time and would have destroyed the purpose of functional duties, which was conservation of limited staff rather than specialization of skill. Other things intervened and I only visited Kumbotso District, which bordered Kano, before another cadet took on this schedule. But with an NA official I did conduct a thorough inspection of the one district council, which had been established some three years earlier.[1]

1. See p. 170 below.

All of us were convinced that we could not possibly do our new jobs without some form of transport. When cadets gathered together in Kano there was usually a very "bolshie" evening or two in the "tenements." These were a row of mud resthouses each consisting of two small unfurnished rooms. There were the luxuries of electric light and a wooden seat over the bucket latrine. Rent was 6*d.* a night. Apart from junior administrative staff the only other regular occupants were the well-diggers and a development officer employed on NA roads. The latter had been a missionary for twenty years or more before joining government. His quiet manner belied immense knowledge and shrewdness about the country. He was very kind to carless cadets, and we always welcomed his presence as it meant easy shopping and an occasional evening at club or cinema. For months he handed on to me his airmail *Times,* taking great pains to get it to me wherever I happened to be.

The well-diggers were a rough crew but great characters. One in particular was a favorite. He would do anything for us, and in return we used to help him draft his innumerable petitions to his headquarters where he was most unjustly regarded as inefficient and unco-operative. He took pride in his work and would never sink a well unless he thought it was necessary and could guarantee success. His wells were the best in the province but his total footage sunk in a month was the lowest in the region. His department was not interested in anything, it seemed, except footage returns, and very few senior engineers ever got around to the inspection of humble village wells. The blue-eyed driller in the province was lazy and overfond of the bottle. He sank easy wells and wasn't worried if they ran dry the first year. For some months he lived in Garki resthouse. The building, some distance from the village, was soon surrounded on all sides by wells. His footage return was excellent, and rumor had it that he had directed all operations from his bed, beer bottle in hand.

Reg, our favorite driller, in filthy shirt and shorts and wearing the jungle hat from which he would never be parted at any time of day or night, sat and listened one evening to our groans. Eventually in a few well-chosen but unprintable words he told us what we should do with the administration from the governor down. Then, typical of his generous nature and despite his unending trouble with his own masters, he offered to try and chauffeur us around the districts where he was working. I did not have to take him up on his offer. I was to remain in Kano for a while and help with the census in the division.

I was given a house, *Gidan* Campbell, empty as a result of all the postings. Mud, three rooms, and sparsely furnished, it seemed like the Ritz. Best of all it had a flat roof on which one could sleep out in the hot season then upon us. Fellow cadets in from tour now stayed with me rather than in the "tenements." When this happened my guest, who arrived complete with servant and camp kit, was allocated a portion of veranda. His servant made him comfortable. At meal times he ate off his crockery with his cutlery. It was friendly, pleasant, and economical—a far cry from the fuss of accommodating guests in small houses once the days of camp kit were past.

Unlike subsequent censuses and elections the 1952 census and the 1951 election were regarded as routine administrative jobs. There were no special appointments or extra payments. The cost of the census, since much maligned, was ½d. per head counted in Northern Nigeria.[2] The Resident was formally gazetted as provincial census officer, and a DO was in general charge but combined it with other duties. I was put onto the job full time. I had one clerk to assist me. With Maitama Sule, then a middle school teacher, I trained the staff of many hundreds required. The division was divided into seven thousand enumeration areas. I prepared nearly all the forms in person and distributed them to the districts. Kano urban area was looked after by the DO himself. The preparatory work occupied me from April to the end of June. Enumeration began on July 7. I went to Kazaure to see how things fared there. The first good rain of the year came down, the census was forgotten, and all went out to plant! However the two weeks allowed in rural areas for the count proved sufficient.

The count over, I set out in a five-ton lorry and visited each of

2. Census Superintendant, *Population Census of the Northern Region of Nigeria 1952* (Zaria: Gaskiya Corporation, 1953), p. 7.

the twenty districts, checking enumerators on the spot and making summaries. I was a hopeless adder after the first hour or so in the morning, and calculating machines were not then usual office equipment. Chance did me a good turn. Adding machines ordered for the Regional Census Office had been sent to Kano by air freight. They traveled on an ill-fated aircraft which made a forced landing in the Sahara. It was some time before the baggage was brought in, and the police sent the machines along to my office. I decided that Kaduna had no use for them until the provinces had finished their work and hung on to the parcel. I was saved hours.

In the middle of all this I received an urgent summons to return to Kano. I imagined something really vital had happened about the census. On arrival I found the other cadets gathered, all agog for the news. Next morning the SDO informed us that he wanted us to assist at the polo tournament which began that afternoon! I dutifully put in an appearance, but next day, with the agreement of the DO in charge of the census, pushed off again. Although there was no desperate hurry I wanted Kano, the largest province, to be the first to finish its count. I was nearly thwarted in this by catching typhoid. For nine days I battled with the census and raging fever, treating myself for malaria. One day I felt so cold I even sat by a fire. After a night in which I woke five or six times soaked through I decided to give up. I was at Wudil, only twenty-five miles from Kano by surfaced road. I had collected and summarized the enumeration sheets from all but three of the districts.

In Kano I was admitted to hospital and fretted away eleven days. The professionalism of doctors has always irritated me but never so much as on this occasion. I assured them that I had treated myself correctly and fully for malaria, but it was three days before anyone would admit that something else might be the matter. When treatment changed I got out my textbook of tropical diseases from under the bed and was able to deduce what was wrong. After a week my opinion was confirmed officially and I was able to take the intelligent interest in recovery which open discussion with the doctors permitted.

The DO in charge of the census collected the papers from the remaining districts and completed his work on the urban area. He and his family were always very kind to me. On secondment from Aden, he did not fit into the hierarchical administrative structure of Northern Nigeria. He was the first senior man to tell me to stop calling him "Sir." (It is interesting that once Nigerians began to enter the service this term of respect was all but universally discarded. Nigerians years my junior called the expatriate head of the service by his first name while I and other expatriates still called him "Sir." In the end we achieved a much more friendly atmosphere on the surface, but depth to it was by no means general.) I suspect that the authoritarian structure of the emirate system had something to do with the way in which the Northern service clung to the mores of the public school. One advanced slowly up the status ladder year by year as new boys arrived. The prefects were very conscious of their position. A junior could break through by good performance on the polo field—and if he made the "school" team he was almost treated as an equal. The South was very different. A Resident from the Western Provinces once said to me on the boat going out to West Africa: "The trouble with the North is that you not only put the women in purdah but the Residents go into it with them." This feeling among officers in the South was general. I took local leave from Kano to stay with a cadet friend at Bamenda in the Cameroons. On arrival I agitated, to my friend's surprise, about signing the Resident's book. Eventually he gave way and we strolled to the imitation German schloss that served as Residency. My friend had no idea where the book was, and hunting about in the grounds for the usual visitors' book shelter we were espied by the Resident. "What the blankety-blank are you up to, Roy?" he shouted. "Come and have a drink." When told I was a cadet from Kano he put on a mock display of deference and had the house turned upside down until the book was found so that it could be graced with so distinguished a signature! I was overwhelmed not only by the strength of his drinks but by his informal hospitality.

To do justice to the Northern service the rather rigid attitude toward protocol was seldom if ever deliberately unkind or hurtful. It seemed essentially absent-minded. Generation followed generation and carried on the traditions bred of a life of great hardship and loneliness in the early days. The postwar intake of ex-servicemen, many with distinguished military careers, brought changes. These were not cadets fresh from school and university but men who had commanded battalions and companies in action. It is significant that a number of them stuck to their titles of rank, quite contrary to their character, just to emphasize to their seniors that they were not schoolboys. The SDO, with whom I had an uneasy relationship and seemed to stick to the older tradition, was not only an able man, but in his way thoughtful and kind to his staff. Now that I was in hospital, for example, he or his wife called most days and kept me supplied with reading matter, and when I was discharged urged me to convalesce in their house. The trouble was that with him I felt like a schoolboy, and I think we all looked upon their hospitality as one would that of a housemaster and his wife, more often a duty than a pleasure. We wore suits to lunch and were never asked to take off our jackets, he called us by our surnames, and she always prefaced our name by a "Mr." This was in marked contrast to the postwar generation of senior officers.

A week after my release from hospital I set off to Kaduna with the several tons of census forms from Kano. It was my first visit to the capital. The road was roundabout, as policy had once decreed that motor roads should not compete with the railway. I cadged a lift with a car owner. We left at 7:15 A.M. and got in at 5:30 P.M., churning through mud and rain most of the way. I was pleased with the Kano census, which I handed over to the Regional Census Officer. There must have been areas where an undercount took place, compounds perhaps not counted at all, but certainly nobody suggested to me that I overcount, and as I made up all the summaries myself, checking each enumeration area result with the annual tax census to spot any wild discrepancies, I would have noticed any attempts to do so at a lower level. Most enumerators were village scribes or schoolboys, and I think we all regarded it as essentially an administrative task. At the level of those of us involved in the work there was little, if any, realization of the possible political implications. I was surprised to find that the 1952 Kano Annual Report not only recorded that the census had the "whole-hearted support of the Native Authorities and was conducted every where with efficiency and accuracy" but that "the claim that well over half the population of Nigeria is in the Northern Region had to be established both for the purposes of representation and for the capitation share of taxes."[3]

In June I took my compulsory examinations, which had to be passed within three years of appointment. The exams were mainly a matter of finding one's way around the index of the particular regulations in which one was being examined. I had hardly looked at the laws before and did not even know there was an examination in *Financial Memoranda,* the bible of treasury procedures. Lower Standard Hausa was taken more seriously. The exam was in two parts, written and oral. I passed the written paper, which was marked centrally. The oral exam was conducted by the Resident. He was keeping up a hallowed tradition. Hermon Hodge records that he was examined by no less a dignitary than His Excellency the Governor.[4] To assist the Resident were two native Hausa speakers of an ilk who would agree with whatever he said. Recently posted to Kano, the Resident had been prevailed upon by some of our allies among the senior officers to modify the rules about car advances. The ineffectiveness of the functional division of duties with transportless cadets was being proved. In other less holy provinces second and even first tour officers were getting advances. He agreed that cadets might be considered for an advance after they had passed their exams. On completion of my oral he announced blandly, "Not bad, but not good enough. We have failed you by one mark." Six months later I took it again. "A big improvement. We have passed you by one mark." I went on leave knowing that I could buy a car. The DO who had been in charge of the census, back in Aden, wrote to me a few months later: "Didn't I hear that you had disgraced yourself by buying a car? In my day no junior officer would have presumed so far!"

My anticipation was, however, of poor consolation to those who

3. A. T. Weatherhead, *Kano Annual Provincial Report, 1952* (Kaduna: Government Printer, 1954), para. 13.
4. *Up against It in Nigeria,* p. 82.

had yet to pass their exams. Christmas found a group of us gathered in the "tenements." A newcomer had musical talent. At lunchtime on Christmas Eve, full of beer, we composed a song taking off our seniors and betters and in a sad refrain lamenting *ad nauseam* our carless state. Cycling back later in the afternoon I had an inspiration as I handed over my machine to the hirer. "Get me six donkeys by eight tonight." In that way Nigerians have of responding to the occasion he delivered the donkeys at the appointed hour. In evening dress we solemnly rode up to the Residency for the office party. Our hostess appeared on the steps to greet us and made the most perfect colonial wife remark of all time: "How very seasonal!" The Resident took it in good part and we later sang our song. Perhaps times were changing, but that was the end of the Northern ju-ju about cars for young officers.

In the emirates Hausa was not only necessary in our day-to-day dealings with ordinary folk who spoke no English. It was the recognized means of communication with all but the most radical NA officials. I often spoke in Hausa to men whose English was much better than my Hausa. Worse, an administrative officer was expected to act as interpreter between visitors and an emir. In some emirates, such as Katsina, where the Emir spoke fluent English with a perfect accent, this seemed a particularly unnecessary homage to the spirit of indirect rule. In later years Nigerian civil servants proved less punctilious, and nearly all, even when native Hausa speakers themselves, preferred to discuss technical and often administrative matters in English. I never succeeded in persuading Hausa-speaking civil servants to compose directly speeches which were to be made in Hausa. They preferred to translate from an English draft. In Kano there was one official, however, to whom we always spoke in English. He was the *Wakilin Waje*, the district head of the *sabon gari*, the quarter of the city where the Southern Nigerians lived. His staff were mainly Southerners and the atmosphere of the office was much more like that of a government than of an NA office. When the *Wakilin Waje* was promoted to a bigger district, the first time I went on tour I greeted him in Hausa as usual, and then switched to English. In Hausa he rebuked me. "We are not in *sabon gari* now," he said. "There I spoke in English for the benefit of those troublesome Southerners, and also to show them that I was as good as they and just as well educated. But here I am among my own people."

✿

The census completed, I was assigned to the adult literacy program. This was one of the imaginative ideas of the new Lieutenant-Governor Sir Bryan Sharwood Smith, who had been my first senior Resident. He had called for a "war on ignorance" to try and stimulate the growth of a public opinion which would be essential to underpin sound political development. Not much progress was achieved, and in mid-1952 administrative officers in each province were appointed to put vigor into the program. We were summoned to a briefing at Zaria, an interesting collection of widely differing ages and lengths of service. A cynic could detect who among the Residents treated the campaign seriously and who thought it a waste of time. One of our number was a "beachcomber" from the Colonial Office to which he was due to return in a couple of months. Another, a fairly senior man from a small province, felt he must be out of favor when he saw that I, the most junior, was from the largest province in population.

Those first years of the campaign were of lasting value. With hardly a primary school per district in the northernmost provinces, adult literacy mattered. We started a campaign which quickly gathered momentum and ought then to have been left to look after itself. People who plant saplings in quantity for fear of loss seldom have the courage to cut out the surplus when the time comes. The growth of all is impaired. This is often the case with good ideas. Some things need ending as well as beginning. Later on the adult literacy campaign was to become institutionalized and stale. It lingered on long after it had outlived its usefulness, controlled by men who had none of the imaginative wisdom of its initiator.

In September I submitted my first report examining the campaign and proposing how it should be stepped up. The rest of my time in Kano was devoted to the literacy campaign. I had given up my house at the end of the census and once again spent most of my time in bush. The NA official responsible had an American pickup. He did not like to spend nights away from Kano, neither did he fancy trekking, so I often took lifts off him and traveled extensively this way. Through him I also found it easier to get NA transport when I needed to hire it. He was a member of the House of Assembly and clearly an up and coming man. People deferred to him and he co-operated well with me. Agricultural shows were becoming popular, and together we established colorful adult education demonstration stalls at every show. These were an instant success and the idea spread to other provinces. One sometimes heard agriculture officers complain that the shows were being taken over by literacy propaganda. At least the presentation of certificates by the emir kept the crowds around, because once the judging of produce and stock was over the unsuccessful farmers tended to seize their exhibits and make off home in ill temper.

My duties covered the whole province, and I was able to visit the Northern Division for the first time. Hadejia, the divisional headquarters was famed for its excellent goose and duck shooting. It was a magnificent sight to see the thousands of birds gathered on the many lakes. With their fringe of reeds and low horizon these reminded me of the smaller Broads in Norfolk. As flight after flight swept over at dusk it was almost impossible to miss. The temptation was to shoot far more than one could dispose of. To stand, gun in hand, as sun went down and moon came up and hear the whistling teals before I could clearly see them was unforgettable. Only the mosquitoes brought me back to reality, and I went home tired and satisfied. There was little game in Kano, the birds were memorable, but the insects made themselves most felt. Hadejia resthouses were full of stinkbugs. These seemed impervious to insecticides, and one could not afford to crush them because of the loathsome smell. The only thing was to make a treaty and hope both sides would leave one another in peace. Buba once made the sad error of filling a pancake with black currant jam in a kitchen with many hundreds of these hard-backed beetles clinging to the ceiling! Another insect pest in Kano was the cantharides beetle, which raised an unpleasant blister from poison injected from its legs. My first acquaintance with it was my worse. I had heard of the beetle but could not yet identify it. One evening my resthouse was full of attractive greenish-black beetles beating themselves against the lamp. I took to my mosquito net to avoid what seemed an innocent nuisance, but not before I had brushed several out of my hair and from the back of my hands. Next morning I knew what had caused the trouble. Never again did I see so many at once. In September each year the earwigs appeared as if by magic. They were everywhere and nipped quite hard when disturbed. Any little hole was an attraction. Each evening as I settled down for a drink, a pipe, and a read I was reminded of their presence. As I squirted the syphon half a dozen fell into my whisky, others lurked in the box of matches, and their brothers hid out by day in the bindings of my books. When the harmattan came they disappeared nobody knows where to.

*

At the end of November I was able to give the Resident a progress report on the establishment of the literacy campaign throughout the province.[5] This report caused some amusement to the cadets. One of our complaints was that we seldom knew what was going on. There was never any organized briefing of us as a group. This could be embarrassing. Some things we picked up from the papers and colleagues in passing. Most of our general information on the new constitution was of this kind. Specific briefing was confined to the conduct of elections. Other things we learned in the worse possible way—from the district heads whose districts we were touring. A particularly bad example of this occurred when the outer council was formed as an intermediary body between the district councils and the native authority council. It so happened that several of us were leaving Kano about the same time. To our surprise we either met the district heads com-

5. See p. 173 below.

ing into Kano or awaiting our arrival to find out what this new council was all about. None of us had any idea and felt both foolish and frustrated in our ignorance.

So two of us made it a practice when in Kano to go along to the office at night, open up the SDO's office (the key hung outside) and read the files on his desk. Our method was furtive but there was nothing secret about what we saw. We just wouldn't have seen it otherwise. Touring officers had no direct contact with the registry. If we asked for the files we were usually told by the Chief Clerk (whose attitude toward junior officers was influenced by the tradition) that they were in action with Resident or SDO and could not be obtained. The new Resident was a great believer in the art of plain English. His marginal comment "pudder" (using, I noticed, a Greek epsilon) was inserted liberally in the margins of letters signed by the mighty in Kaduna as well as upon drafts submitted by his own staff. We found on one of our nocturnal visits to the office a letter from the Resident to the Civil Secretary asking for twelve copies of Sir Ernest Gowers' *Plain Words* to be sent immediately, as he was appalled to find junior officers in the province using such jargon as "unilateral action." To our delight we subsequently discovered that the phrase causing the pother had been drafted by the SDO. It was therefore all the more amusing to find that the Resident praised my progress report not for its content but for its freedom from pudder!

*

At the end of January, 1953, I left Kano by air on leave. I had enjoyed my tour and was to enjoy my leave, the first time I had ever been in England with money to spare in my pocket. I felt I had learned quite a lot and achieved something, though not as much as I would have done if the frustrations had been fewer. There is no doubt that our life as cadets was all but dominated by our irritation at lack of transport. My development officer friend once said to me: "In a few years' time you will be looking back on these days wishing you could have them all over again." Years later, he called into my office when I was deputy to the head of the service and daily sitting on a razor's edge of political delicacy.

He was still in bush, making the excellent roads for which he was renowned. I reminded him of his remark made one pleasant evening together in Kibiya resthouse, and told him how right he had been. But at the time we were in a difficult period of transition. In many ways I hankered after the past. I would have liked to have been an ADO twenty years earlier, but in 1951 we had to keep up with change taking place all round us. We were not only young men, but had been brought up in a different world from many of our seniors. Above all we had to make our career not in the old Nigeria but in the new. We felt we should be trusted more and made to feel part of a team rather than inexperienced subordinates with limited value. Kano, so big and important and full of problems, was a special case, for other provinces seemed much better in this respect. In these was less work in some ways, and a smaller staff. The remoter the station the more friendly it usually was. But Kano NA itself was the biggest, and the Emir the highest-paid man in the country, governor included. I envied my colleagues who had been posted to divisions where a cadet was perhaps one of only two administrative staff. They learned much more much faster, were known by the people, and could do something useful. In later years I was often to grieve over the loss to the service of first-class men who had been put off by first tours in Kano. It was a bad place to begin.

Part 3. Assistant District
Officer, Zaria Division

While on leave I was posted to Zaria Province to replace an officer transferred to Kano after the riots of May, 1953. I was not sorry. I had liked what little I had seen of Zaria during the Special Duties Officers' Conference, and I had always preferred the southern part of Kano which was adjacent to Zaria with its denser vegetation and rocky hills to the flat and sandy northern districts. I traveled from England by sea taking a car with me. The drive north from Lagos was almost entirely on laterite roads, and I spent two nights on the way. Ibadan to Bida was a full day's journey because of the slow ferry crossing at Wuya during the rains. From Bida to Zaria the narrow road wound through the hills and crossed hundreds of streams bridged in the simplest fashion with a few planks. From Zungeru to Funtua by old Birnin Gwari I passed not a single vehicle. In 1953 the railway was still the main transport between north and south in marked contrast to a few years later. Nowadays Lagos to Zaria can be covered in one hard day's driving, all on a good tarmac surface.

Although Zaria and Kano were neighboring provinces the difference in atmosphere was at once noticeable. Zaria lacked the commercial bustle of Kano, the native authority was poorer, and there was little evidence of development except in government-sponsored education. The administration was as sleepy as the province. Whereas "fliers" were chosen to lead Kano Province, "have beens" were often quietly bedded down in Zaria. Kaduna, the regional capital, was part of the province. To be Resident, I was told by an Irish missionary, was as bad as being parish priest to an archbishop. Whereas in Kano cadets became frustrated because they felt they were kept out of the picture, in Zaria the frustration was caused by there being no picture. New men were seized upon to "filter files," of which I had never seen so few. I found myself one of several sitting around less than half occupied in the badly sited divisional office, nearly four miles from the city and the native authority. Of the junior administrative staff, one had a busy job in the treasury; another looked after the pathetic little enclave directly administered as a township; in Kaduna there was a township worth administering, and this was the job of the third; a fourth had, to me the enviable, touring area of southern Zaria. We seldom saw the local authority in charge of Kaduna Township. He was very much at the beck and call of the potentates of the Secretariat. The touring officer too was cut off because of distance. In the rains he was three hundred miles away on bad roads.

At first, however, I enjoyed my new status. I was no longer a "new boy." I had a house and a car. I possessed an independence which had never been mine in Kano. But I soon tired of lack of work, and I longed to get out and see what promised to be an interesting and beautiful province. I suggested to the SDO that I go on tour in what seemed to me the rarely toured northern part of the division. His reply became a classic quote in the service: "What do you want to do that for? Somebody went on tour last month. Oh, no! There are far too many files here already. Your job is to keep some of them off." He smiled blandly over his empty desk and shortly afterward went home to listen to the latest cricket scores. Just as the Resident had a Lieutenant-Governor too close for comfort, so the SDO had the Resident on top of him all the time, because there was only one division in the province. Inevitably the Resident ran the division, so the SDO had less work than usual quite apart from his temperament. Most of my fellows had long since been demoralized, and the weak starters had the worse brought out in them. One, after five months in the division, still did not know the way to the NA office. He left that side of things to the ADO in the treasury.

Somebody went on leave and I was switched from the divisional to the provincial office. The distinction between the two in Katsina and Zaria provinces was ridiculous because within the provinces there was only one division, but it, like the small directly administered Zaria Township, was an administrative monstrosity which nobody of sufficient seniority ever had the imagination or the courage to change. Later on we several times managed to rationalize the administrative structure in Zaria, only to be thwarted in our streamlining of work and reduction of staff by headquarters posting "difficult cases" to be either DO provincial office or local authority. As I grew up I better appreciated the convenience, and indeed the occasional necessity, of sinecures, but I never accepted their location as a burden on a small province. My new duties were no more arduous, but the Resident was more energetic than the SDO. For the first time I tried my hand at drafting letters and reports which were destined for higher places. When a rocket came through about the poor response to the adult literacy campaign in the province I exploited my Kano experience and got myself appointed special duties officer on condition that it did not disturb my office work. My motive was largely selfish. I wanted some kind of excuse to get out on tour and see the province. I bided my time carefully. Four and a half months after arrival I made use of a public holiday combined with a weekend to visit some literacy classes and step up the campaign. Even the Resident could not dash the youthful enthusiasm behind such a move. For the next sixth months I worked hard at adult literacy and before handing over to a specialist in April, 1964, was able to report reasonable progress.[6]

❋

One of the problems of working for the Resident was the opportunities it provided, unless one was careful, of working for his wife. She was a rather status-conscious Bostonian, the only hostess I ever knew who produced a table plan when there were only six of us dining. Wives of senior officials were expected to organize "good works." The pendulum swung in Northern Nigeria between the Red Cross and the Girl Guides, depending largely on the interests of the first lady at Government House. One day the Resident rather diffidently asked me to get in touch with his wife, who required a "little help." I found myself stand-

6. See p. 177 below.

ing on the back of the office lorry in the city and *sabon gari* markets for several hours every morning for a week selling raffle tickets! I received a letter of thanks for the "yeoman services" I had rendered couched in dignified but charming language. The raffle made £700 for the Red Cross but, like most charitable affairs in colonial territories, at considerable cost to the unidentified taxpayer who, on this occasion, among other expenses had lost the best part of a week's work from me.

✿

The lack of touring, residence in a town, and my new mobility gave me opportunities to branch out socially in a way life in Kano Province had prohibited. Two older men in particular had a great influence on my future attitudes. Both lived in semiseclusion away from the government station and were regarded as somewhat eccentric by fellow Europeans. Both had a great love for Nigeria and were shrewd assessors of the contemporary scene. I loved to listen to their anecdotes of the past. Captain Money, a retired DO, held court to innumerable Nigerians from the Clerical Training Center (which grew into the Institute of Administration) and the other places of learning which Zaria boasted. He was an institution in the home towns of some of these students. One day a young man burst in whom he had never seen before. "Who are you? I don't know you," was the blunt inquiry which gave no offense both because of the speaker's reputation for kindness and his obvious sympathy. "You don't know me, but you hanged my father," came the disconcerting reply fortunately accompanied by a beaming smile.

For a long time DO at Idoma, my friend took a delight in telling young Idomas his outrageous and apochryphal version of how they got their customs. In the twenties the government had become very anthropologically minded and administrators anxious to make a reputation had thrown themselves into investigation of lineage, kith and kin, marriage and burial customs of the peoples in their divisions. The man in Idoma, according to Guy Money, had spoken no Idoma and the Idomas were in any case not at all communicative about intimate domestic details. However the DO had an excellent Hausa interpreter with an inventive turn of mind. Seeing how desperately anxious his master was to record every custom, the garrulous old man filled in the many gaps left by the obstinate Idomas with his own imagination. Everyone was happy. The Idomas kept their secrets to themselves, the DO made page upon page of notes, and the interpreter was praised for his ardent help. The "customs" were thus recorded, analyzed, and finally drafted into an imposing manual entitled *The Customs of the Idoma*. Thereafter whenever a marriage dispute was referred to the DO he would consult the recorded wisdom of his anthropologically minded predecessor and give judgment accordingly. So, bit by bit, such was the awe in which the book was held by all parties, the inventions of the Hausa interpreter became accepted as the genuine customs of the people! When Captain Money died in 1954 hundreds turned up to his funeral. His body lies in an unmarked grave at his own request in the country he loved more than his own.

The other man, Wilfrid Jeffries, was head of a literature agency which was formed to produce something for the newly literate to read. Between them they taught me the most important lessons which I had to learn and helped give me the armor of cynicism which was essential protection to the delicate mechanism of sympathy. They showed me how much there was to do and how pointless it was to battle away at immovable obstacles. It was always better to turn aside and devote one's energies to something else equally worthwhile but, because it was attainable, of greater immediate value. They reminded me that my indignation over apparent injustice was probably much greater than that of those intimately affected. In 1906 Hermon Hodge had sighed, "It is almost useless trying to help the oppressed. The peasant is fair game, not only in the eyes of others, but in his own."[7] In 1953 it was very different but it was still true that village life would be very dull without any corruption or scandal, that it was more important to change the system than to pursue individuals. "Your job is to keep people out of prison, not to put them in," I was

7. *Up against It in Nigeria*, p. 102.

firmly told when I once announced triumphantly that I thought I had the skids under a corrupt official.

Neither attempted to instruct me about relationships with Africans whose presence as visitors in a European household was still rare in 1953. But by precept I learned how quiet patience and simplicity were essential if I was to make contact. It seems strange now how difficult it then appeared. When my wife first joined me she stayed in a Nigerian home within a week of arrival without any consciousness. But in the early fifties such contact as existed, and it was very formal, was usually between administrative officers and the local aristrocracy. There was, of course, a substantial difference in social status between the average Englishman and the average Nigerian. For example, Nigerians of my own age and with education such as might produce some interests in common would usually be junior civil servants or schoolteachers. Quite apart from race there would be a wide gap in earning capacity and standards of living. My few attempts at friendship with such people in Kano had been unsuccessful. I was looking for companionship and some kind of intellectual understanding in a rather lonely life. Followers, in the Northern tradition of *fadanci*,[8] were not what I wanted, but what I usually got. In the provincial office at Zaria were a number of clerks with secondary education, and tentatively I began to try and get to know some of them as people rather than just as employees. It was not easy. I was embarrassed if other Europeans found Nigerians in my house. Either the European decided not to stay or the Nigerian melted away at his approach. At very best the two Europeans talked uneasily while the Nigerian sat silent, endlessly and unseeingly turning over the pages of a magazine. The whole savored of the secrecy required, because of the presence of so many expatriate wives, of liaisons with Nigerian mistresses. But whereas I had quickly despaired in Kano, I found courage to persevere in Zaria. There were colleagues and friends trying to do the same thing, and year by year it became more natural and simpler until the present, when, if there is no contact, it is be-

8. Paying homage at the court of an emir, patronage seekers.

cause it is not desired on the part of one side or the other. The colonial situation is not, of course, conducive to easy social relationships between master and subject, and independence makes an enormous psychological difference. But the fifties were merely the culminating point of many years of contact in which good and honest colonial civil servants had slowly built up the trust and confidence which men of my generation were able to exploit.

Those who have only known Nigeria since independence may find it hard to accept that social relationships in the fifties could present problems. How important such slight and brief acquaintanceships as we had could be to individual Nigerians can be shown in this extract from a letter sent to me by a clerk in my office while I was on leave.

I am confident that you are enjoying your leave. UK certainly is now in the grip of election "fever." All, I imagine, is astir. A great deal of hustle and bustle there? To which side do you suppose the wind will blow this time? I shall appreciate your effort to inform me of the trend of events over there.

A lot has been missed since you left. Who knows whether or not the loss will continue. Now I am in the dark about world affairs. There is nothing for it, however. The only prayer is that you may come back to Zaria.

The writer of the letter, like most of the office staff, was a Southerner, but in Zaria there was a wide cross-section of Northern peoples. By chance I met one of my own age about to go to England for higher studies. We got to know one another and our respective families well and have remained good friends. Slowly over the years through the warmth of this friendship I began to acquire the understanding I needed of the people among whom I worked.

On a more formal level I joined the Zaria Youths' Literary and Debating Society. I had been a guest speaker, enjoyed the evening, and applied for membership. Intellectually the society was not exactly stimulating, but I welcomed the way in which I was treated as an equal—neither placed on a lofty white pedestal nor excluded by use of vernacular from the more intimate conversations. Contacts made at the weekly meetings were often to be renewed in all sorts of circumstances, sometimes tragic. Men whose faces and names I had long forgotten would greet me in the streets of Lagos or Ibadan. I would get an easy passage through customs or immigration. Once I was asked to support an admission to the Inns of Court. In the troubled times of 1966 I was able to help save the life of a fellow member, while another, a clerk I had persuaded to join the army, by this time promoted lieutenant colonel, was sadly killed by his own men.

✿

With a fellow ADO I got involved in scouting. I had enjoyed my days as a scout, and although I doubted the validity in an African setting of scouting methods, the philosophy was sound and I could not be blind to the boys' enthusiasm. A couple of expatriate helpers with transport at their command gave the movement in Zaria a substantial boost. We had to be wary of the dangers of being too generous of time and cars. One was always getting surprises. On a wet and stormy afternoon I gave a lift unasked to a young man who was obviously stuck on the open road a long way from shelter. I dropped him inside the town. We did not speak, and, concentrating on driving through the heavy rain, I did not register his appearance. A few days later a stranger came to my door beaming smiles of recognition. When I did not respond he explained that he was "the boy whom you picked in your car." An applicant, he had spent the intervening time tracing me as a possible patron for had I not demonstrated my "love" for him by an unsolicited lift?

Scouts luckily were too young to become a nuisance, although their scouters, rather a curious group of men, often were. The latter preferred committee meetings to camp and tended to use their uniforms to obtain free entry to football matches on the Saturday afternoons I could spare for activities, for both of which mercies I was duly thankful. The delight of taking town boys to bush, something I had never foreseen, more than repaid my efforts. Their uproarious laughter at the sight of a monkey, their sense of achievement—surely equalling Scott's at the Pole or Hillary's on Everest—when they forded a river or climbed a steep hill, and their rapid and friendly (and quite non-tribal) fun together as I kept quietly in the background gave joy to many a holiday.

Some years later I came across an article in a secondary school magazine. The two English scouts were my colleague and myself. We got a week's local leave just before Christmas and took as many of the Zaria scouts as we could pack into a railway coach to camp. We stayed on to enjoy a quiet but delightful Christmas in one of the nicest villages in Nigeria, a tradition we have kept up through many years.

The Adventures of a Young Scout

On a cold harmattan evening in December 1954 my grandmother had a visitor. It was my scoutmaster, come to implore her to let me accompany other Zaria scouts on a camping expedition to Kagoro (near Kafanchan), many miles away from home. She was not easily persuaded but eventually, after receiving definite promises that I would be well looked after, she gave her consent.

What an opportunity for me!—a tiny little boy to accompany secondary school boys! I had previously been on only one short local camp and so now considered myself the luckiest boy in the world; even the cold harmattan weather could not discourage me. I had a week to wait before the day of our departure and that week seemed like a whole year to me.

The day came round at last. Accompanied by two English scouts, we journeyed to Kafanchan by rail and then on to the Kagoro camp site by road. A meal—of boiled yams and palm oil—was ready for us when we arrived. This we devoured gratefully, had a rest, and then set to work. Our first task was to build shelters for ourselves and so we went in search of suitable branches; it was at this time that we killed two enormous deadly snakes, both of which I was the first to observe. We erected four shelters, three on one side of the river and one on the other (the camp site straddled a river); three, including the isolated one, for scouts and one for scoutmasters.

Our first camp-fire was held in the evening of the same day. Some boys, one at each shelter, had to be left on guard but they got their chance to attend other camp-fires later. On this occasion—and during every other camp-fire during the week—we enjoyed the companionship of the villagers, who listened to our songs and, in their turn, entertained us with their own native music.

Early in the mornings we freshened ourselves up by swimming in the river. Even the cold weather did not deter us although the smaller boys, like myself, were content to remain in the shallower parts. In the course of the day many scouting activities were carried out to improve our knowledge, our skill, and our scouting classification.

And of course, I must mention the cable bridge which linked the solitary shelter on the far side of the river with the main party. It was, at first, an awe-inspiring experience to cross the river on this swinging bridge; one felt suspended in space and waited in horror to find oneself hurtling through the air to certain death on the rocks beneath. For the first two days we were reluctant to use the bridge but eventually familiarity bred contempt and we youngsters began to treat it as a swing! The villagers had to warn us about the danger we were facing.

For the preparing of meals boys in each shelter worked together; everyone played his part. At night we heard the villagers scraping our cooking pots, which had been left outside, for the remains of our food.

Two days before the end of the camp we climbed the Kagoro Rock. This was a difficult and dangerous climb; indeed, one of our scout-masters was nearly killed by a rolling rock. We drank some of the clear cool water from the stream flowing down the rock and then returned—with much less difficulty than we went.

Then our wonderful week of camping came to an end. We played a football match against the Kagoro youths (which we lost), bade farewell to the villagers, thanked the chief for all the help he had given us to make our stay a pleasant one, and returned to Zaria.

And wasn't my grandmother pleased to see me back again, safe and sound!

M. MOHAMMED
Form II

✿

The administration in Zaria began to look up. Personnel changed as officers went on leave and others were posted in their place. Before long I found, as I had at Kano, a group of go-ahead and enthusiastic ADO's as my colleagues. The top remained somnolent for a while longer, but the man who had nursed me on first arrival at Kazaure was in the division, kept things moving, and acted as a useful buffer when occasion demanded. Over the next three years what became known as the "ADO's Union" exercised an influence on affairs out of all proportion to the experience and knowledge of its members. Ignoring our masters whenever we could, we gaily did things in their name. Never had so many letters, unseen and unapproved, left a province signed "for Resident." Very rarely, and then only when language had been too youthfully arrogant, did we get a comeback. For a few days Resident and SDO would rouse themselves, but soon sank back into reverie content that the work was getting done at little trouble to themselves. Indeed more than work was getting done; at last some progress was being made. The Nigerian junior staff were split in much the same way as the administrative officers. Two elderly chief clerks, one of whom knew the numbers and titles of over five thousand files by heart but had no understanding of their contents, fitted in well with Zaria traditions. They resented us and our alliance with those of the junior clerks who were keen to learn and be given responsibility. Cautious respect was always evident, but the finance clerk was shrewd enough to handle our salaries and allowances with commendable despatch while quietly embezzling part of the Resident's for over a year before detection.

I was learning far more about practical administrative problems and government procedures than I had in Kano. We saw all the mail and kept one another informed. The fun soon overcame the frustrations. Much of our activity centered on promoting the welfare of southern Zaria, more than half the emirate and comprising non-Hausa, non-Moslem peoples living in subjection to Zaria Native Authority. Three independent districts and three emirate districts formed the parish of a touring officer based at Zonkwa. He fought a never ending battle to get action on the innumerable problems arising in an area where the traditionally subject pagan peoples were rapidly adopting Christianity and acquiring Western education. The Provincial Annual Report of 1954, beginning with that fearful cliché of so many of its fellows: "The year to be reviewed was one of steady if unspectacular progress," spoke rather naïvely and complacently of the situation, partly to avoid giving offense, but did reveal its seriousness.

Affairs in southern Zaria, including the non-Moslem districts of Zaria Emirate and the non-Moslem independent districts of Moroa, Kagoro, and Jaba, have called for special attention during the year. Encouraged by recent political developments, the demands, particularly from the younger, semi-educated sections of the Kaje and Katab tribes, for separation from Zaria Emirate and the formation of a distinct, independent Administrative Division of Southern Zaria to include the present independent districts and the non-Moslem districts of Zaria Emirate, became more vocal and more intense. These demands were accompanied by sweeping allegations of maladministration, neglect and suppression all in general terms and rarely, if ever, supported by specific complaints brought forward by the individuals claiming to have been injured. Although it would be idle to pretend that the administration of this area is perfect I do not believe that it is worse than in most other parts of Nigeria and it is an historical fact that the administration of this area is perfect I do not believe that it people have developed in recent years from a jumble of savage, interfighting households and hamlets into peaceful cohesive administrative units which have been taught to take an ever increasing part in the conduct of their own affairs. The charge of neglect is also demonstrably false, though it must of course be admitted that a vast amount of development has still to be effected, here as elsewhere. Indeed, it is true to say that it is largely because of the extent and speed with which this area has been developed that the present situation has arisen.

In the first quarter of the present century the main administrative problem in Southern Zaria was to get the local people to take any interest in their own public affairs but this has now largely been overcome. In this connection it is relevant to note that the 1952 Census has shown that more than 5.6% of the population of Zaria Province is literate in Roman script: this is more than double the figure for the whole Region (2.1%) and is closely approached only by Ilorin (5.4%), Plateau (5.1%), and Kabba (4.7%) Provinces. In view of the larger number of schools and the smaller proportion of provincial population in the southern than in the northern area of Zaria Province, it is safe to say that the percentage of literacy in Southern Zaria must be considerably higher than the provincial percentage and that it is probably the highest percentage for any area of comparable size in the Northern Region. As a result of this development instead of the early lack of interest there has now arisen in this area, especially among the younger and more literate generation, these urgent demands for a greater share in the management of their local affairs, greater decentralisation, more development of every kind and, in the Emirate Districts, the substitution of an indigenous District administration for the existing system.

Although the local people are not yet capable of assuming the responsibilities which they ask to be given to them now, their demands have been given sympathetic consideration and, in consultation with the Regional Government, plans have been made to ensure that the political and material development of the area can be carried out as rapidly as possible. His Honour has agreed to post to Zaria Province in January 1954 a Senior District Officer with special qualifications who will be stationed at Zonkwa in Southern Zaria and who will be assisted by a second Administrative Officer also based on Zonkwa. These officers, in collaboration with Native Authorities, District Heads and the local people, will be responsible for all types of development in the area and especially for building up the Village, District and Area Councils into efficient and democratic Local Government organisations. Plans have also been made to establish at Zonkwa a Sub-Treasury of Zaria Native Treasury and branches of other NA departments: this should much reduce the delay and inconvenience which has been caused to those in Southern Zaria by the great distance separating them from the Central Treasury and Offices in Zaria.[9]

This sudden burst of interest and energy, important as it was for southern Zaria, begged a number of questions. There were four districts north of the six in southern Zaria which were equally non-Moslem and non-Hausa. These had never been included in the Zonkwa touring area and had been far less influenced by Christian missions. Little was heard about them or from them and they were wrongly left out of the overall plan. I had no chance of going to Zonkwa but my interest had been aroused by the "middle belt" of the division, the more so as the map was largely blank. A letter of complaint came in one day from a village called Kono. I was unable to find it on the map. The cheerful and resourceful head messenger located it in the center of the blank area on the map. He spoke of high hills, savage people, murders, and boundary disputes. No one had been there, he thought, since before the war. Mountains—and not a contour on the map. I resolved to go and see for myself; meanwhile I read what there was in anthropological books and divisional files. In January, 1954, I was back in the division and for a few weeks we were overflowing with staff. I slipped off, promising to be back within the week, but I knew that once I was in the hills there could be no recall. I had already made a preliminary trip between Christmas and the New Year to Kauru, the district headquarters. I spent time in Kauru and visited all the Hausa villages on the plains so that on a second visit honor would have been satisfied when I asked to go into the hills.[10]

Kauru, a former independent kingdom, was attractively situated around two rocky hills. The chief's compound was huge and old, and like many others of its kind dominated by a vast silk-cotton tree which could be seen for miles around. I took out a radio set just purchased by the district council, and while I was in Kauru the death of the Emir of Kano was announced. The aged *Sarkin Kauru*, when he heard, accepted that the radio (the first set he had been able to handle and listen to at leisure) was more than a new type of gramophone! I saw my first hill pagans. My diary records: "Large crowd of Rumaiya in Kauru selling (?) corn to the NA. Women nude except for colorful chastity belts and bangles on arms and legs. Men mainly in Hausa dress, boys with fancy haircuts. I saw some pleasant, frank looking faces."

On investigation I discovered the truth about the corn. The non-Hausa peoples were assessed, along with tax, so many measures of corn, which they had to sell to the NA at less than market price. Those defaulting were fined. The corn was taken to Zaria and stored as an emergency famine relief supply. The country had plenty of experience of poor harvests and locust devastation. An emergency corn supply was a sound scheme. Bigger and wealthier native authorities than Zaria tended to buy corn through contractors, a system wide open to abuse, with ridiculously high prices often paid for both corn and transport. Zaria bought direct from the farmers and justified the imposition of the burden on pagans only on the grounds that they paid less tax than Hausa farmers and needed encouragement to grow more food crops. This I might have been able to swallow were it not for the fact that the corn was in practice sold off, in the absence of famine, on credit at the purchase price to NA employees, of whom the Emir was the biggest buyer. Credit was continuous and, because of the eminence of those involved, neither redeemed nor refused. It took two years' hard work to end this

10. See p. 181 below.

obnoxious practice which by the mid-fifties offered wonderful potential for political exploitation.

"Non-Hausa peoples" is an awkward phrase. The Hausas themselves referred to pagans without hesitation and, alas, usually with contempt. It was hard for us to avoid the word "pagan," for in Zaria alone there were some forty indigenous peoples with language, culture, and religion of their own. But if we called them pagans it was not in a derisory sense. Southern Zaria quickly captured the hearts of those who worked there. The ADO's Union were pagans to a man. The two weeks I spent in the Kauru hills that January remain the greatest touring experience of my service, and perhaps the time most well spent. The contrast to staying in Hausa villages was immense. There was no efficient touring team as in Kano, few if any preparations were made in advance, and there was far less respect for either DO or NA as institutions. One got a lodging, but of privacy there was none. Some villagers came out miles in all their number to meet you, others refused to provide carriers so that you could stay longer. Young men showed little respect for their elders or my retinue. If I was willing to talk so were they. They sat around me all day and watched and commented on all I did. They did not address me *ranka ya dade,* the Hausa term of respect for a senior, but *maigida,* the term for the head of a household, or simply as DO. They climbed up hilltops with me, showed me all I wanted to see. In one village when I did at last get to bed outside the hut that was my temporary home several of the most talkative lay down on either side, providing my slumbers with a bodyguard under the beautiful starlit sky.

I was lucky in my messenger during this and many subsequent treks in southern Zaria. Malam Arzika came from Birnin Kebbi in Gwandu Emirate in Sokoto Province. He had served in the army during the war and had reached the rank of sergeant before his discharge. His great hero was the saintly Emir of Gwandu, Yahaya, who more than any other Nigerian chief during British rule displayed all the virtues of kingship and practiced none of the vices. Arzika emulated his hero. He was kind, patient, and incorruptible. His patience with difficult young mission adherents, whose insecurity often made them unpleasantly aggressive and even abusive in laying their complaints, far exceeded mine. Each evening he quietly picked out those in the village whom he felt required special attention and brought them to me next morning: an ex-serviceman and Burma veteran wanting his war medals and, if possible, employment (and who to this day is my steward); a boy who had managed so far in some school but was stuck for further progress through lack of funds; a man trained in laying monkey poison but never employed; and so on. It was paradoxical that a Fulani should assist in disclosing so many of the inadequacies of the Fulani-Hausa rule of pagan peoples and show such concern for them as human beings. I blessed Arzika and my good fortune and thought how different Northern Nigeria might have been had fifty Yahayas reigned in fifty emirates for fifty years.

Sarkin Kauru I found more of an ally than I would have expected. He was a Habe district head, successor to the former Chiefs of Kauru, and therefore not "in" with the emir and the native authority. Kauru, along with the other former vassal states of Kajuru and Kagarko now incorporated into the emirate as districts, remained outside the true political society of Zaria.[11] They could be neglected with comparative impunity. Kauru was the most neglected of all, Kajuru running a close second. Kagarko came within the Zonkwa touring area and had therefore gained from effective British supervision. To *Sarkin Kauru* I might prove the means to better the lot of his kingdom and of himself. He and *Sarkin Kajuru*, for example, were the only two district heads without cars. They were refused salary advances on the grounds that their emoluments, the lowest of all district heads, could not stand the necessary repayments, and that their districts had so few roads. Logical and reasonable arguments, which would be likely to appeal to the British administrator who would sense with pleasure a growing appreciation of financial responsibility by the NA. But they begged the question. Smaller and far less difficult districts whose control was a Fulani preserve carried higher salaries. Just as in Kano I had found I could achieve more in the Habe district of Rano, so in Zaria I found that I could guarantee much

11. M. G. Smith, *Government in Zazzau*, p. 279.

more positive support from the Habe district heads. In Lere, a neighboring district similar to Kauru, the *Wali* was a Fulani aristocrat and candidate to the throne. He had absolutely no interest in his district. He had not even bothered, such was his expectation of promotion elsewhere, in twenty-two years as district head and the only car-owner in the area, to improve the nine miles of road between Lere and Saminaka sufficiently to allow him to drive out of the district during the rains. At best the *Wali* gave one passive co-operation, while *Sarkin Kauru* threw himself into projects with a will despite his advanced years and long experience of failure.

Together, and with the help of colleagues and in particular of the ADO who followed me in the area, we slowly implemented the various proposals in my first touring report. To get money for the roads I proposed necessitated the creation of a phony settlement scheme. But the road to Kwasam was built and a cotton market established at the end of it. The momentum these two developments gave to the economy of the area enabled it to take off and keep moving forward on its own. Ten years later it flourished. The villages, with but few exceptions, were no longer in the hills, and the attraction was less, but it was good to see the people so prosperous and better able to compete in a society in which they traditionally remained second-class citizens.

Some eight years after my first visit I went into the hills again with a group of Nigerian administrative officers in training. Their task was to carry out an economic survey and help plot village names on an aerial survey map which had just been completed. They stayed in pairs among the various tribes, and I moved from place to place enjoying once again the pleasures of trekking and the freedom of the mountains. I spent a night in Kiballo, the loneliest of all the villages and the most backward of the peoples, with the chief and elders still clinging to their rocks. My students, a Kano Hausa and a Gombe Fulani, were not altogether comfortable in the unaccustomed and unsophisticated surroundings. We chatted in the evening to the old men, some of whom spoke no Hausa and had never traveled farther than Rishiwa, five miles away. We tested their knowledge of current affairs. Kaduna, the Northern Peoples' Congress, the Premier were unknown to them. Then one old, old man had a dim recollection of a great overlord from the outside world who had come and gone but no doubt still ruled his domains elsewhere. I asked the name. "Dan Giwa," came the reply, the nickname of Captain Ffrench, the British officer who led the 1907 patrol into the hills. I commented to my students that independence seemed to have gone unnoticed among the Kiballo. "Boy!" one of them replied, "they haven't even heard of the British Empire yet!"

❀

The toughest problem in trying to bring along southern Zaria was finding employment for those with primary or secondary education. The NA was virtually closed to pagans.[12] One had to have heard the contempt put into the Hausa phrase *su arna,* "those pagans," to appreciate how intense feelings were.[13] These were people from whom slaves had been found until very recently. In any case appointment into the service of the NA was less a matter of "merit or technical qualifications [than governed] . . . by ties of loyalty in a situation of political rivalry where the stakes are considerable."[14] There was no shame about the accepted reality. That this should have been the case in the first decade of the twentieth century, even in the twenties and thirties, I could understand. In the fifties, with independence on the doorstep, it was monstrous, and I and the others of my colleagues involved in southern Zaria could not accept it complacently. My efforts in Kauru were naturally unpopular with the NA, but they were a beginning, and pressure from the excellent administrator appointed to Zonkwa began to have an effect there too. The

12. See the figures for ethnic employment in Zaria NA in 1950, *ibid.,* p. 273.
13. The Minorities Commission rather unfairly dismissed this feeling with the comment: "As to expressions of contempt, we do not suppose that they are used only by Muslims, nor is Northern Nigeria the only place where people speak contemptuously of each other" (Nigeria, *Report of the Commission Appointed to Enquire into the Fears of Minorities and the Means of Allaying Them,* hereafter cited as *Minorities Commission Report.* Cmnd. 505, July, 1958, p. 59).
14. M. G. Smith, *Government in Zazzau,* p. 288.

majority of educated men, however, found employment outside the NA—especially in the Nigeria Police and the army, unpopular employment with the Hausa-Fulani elite. The full significance of this was to be discovered only in 1966 when the southern Zarians and other similar minority peoples were found together to be the majority of the fighting men in the army.

Our early efforts to break open the NA service were often frustrated by the southern Zarians themselves not settling down or quickly giving cause for complaint. All too often they relied not only on European patronage to get them into employment but to keep it for them whatever their performance. It was impossible to convince them of the vulnerability of their position and how each failure (and there were many) put back our plans. I became instrumental in this matter of employment when I was given the finance schedule. This involved close supervision of the NA treasury and staff matters, and I sat on many NA committees, including the Appointments Committee. I quickly made allies among some of the staff by promoting their own welfare. Salaries had not kept pace with recent facilities for training, and trained staff were at a premium elsewhere. I was then more able to set about pushing things on behalf of Kauru and for the SDO in Zonkwa. His task was extremely difficult. His position, an imposition by the regional government, was resented by the Emir, who knew southern Zaria well, having long been a district head there, and was not eased by the sluggish leadership of the provincial administration.

The sub-NA was a compromise which required good will and co-operation to succeed. But communications were poor: no telephone, bad roads, a slow and indifferent mail service. The Emir usually had the first and the last word in the inevitable disputes. He could pick up his phone and speak to the Resident. The SDO had to drive two hundred miles. For many months I acted virtually as a secret agent for the SDO, following up matters which my seniors preferred for one reason or another to ignore. Just how bad the situation was can be seen from a letter to me, in reply to a private note I had sent concerning the removal, without consultation, of southern Zaria projects from an estimate of how to spend the annual allocation for road and market improvements.

Very many thanks for your note about roads and markets. I very nearly burst a blood-vessel when I read it. The score is mounting up against Zaria! One day I will say what I think, it will include a host, but it will not include you who seem to me to be the only person who either co-operates or talks honestly and gives a straight answer even if it is sometimes NO.

I incidentally wired the Resident personally about two weeks ago about this very matter. Stony silence since.

Personally I am sorry that I subscribe my name officially to keeping Southern Zaria in the Province/Emirate. It could not be worse even if it was attached to Jema'a.

On re-reading this compromising note it would appear that I am frustrated and depressed. Frustrated, yes—it does not work to combine the powers of a Touring Officer with the authority of an SDO—depressed, no, I only get official humbug and "smarm" on paper!

Luckily changes were eventually made in Zaria too, and the SDO and his successor, another outstanding man handpicked for the job, were able to make much more progress and not have to resort to intriguing with a junior ADO. Alas, as British control passed to Nigerian, Zaria NA began once again to assert itself, and with a close political alliance between the new emir (appointed in 1959) and the premier, the Zonkwa sub-NA was closed down and administrative officers no longer posted there on a permanent basis.

Some of the southern Zaria men whom we had forced upon the NA and who had survived the hazards of employment, influenced by the Hausa society of Zaria and anxious for an alternative security to British protection, took the public step of rejecting Christianity for Islam. Legislators elected on the platform of the United Middle Belt Congress in opposition to the establishment followed suit. They first crossed the floor to the NPC and then to Islam. To the majority of their people these steps were seen as a great betrayal. But the Christian missions continued to thrive in southern Zaria and after the withdrawal of the British became the greatest external influence.

It is only a matter of time before the traditional Zaria overlords face a revolt. They rejected the chance of compromise and the opportunity for integration. The NA has not kept pace with the other agencies for development. In southern Zaria it is more than the conflict between old and young, illiterate and educated, common to many parts of the North. It is also the revolt of a slave population against its former masters.

Despite the failure of so many of the southern Zarians to come up to the unfairly high expectations we had of them there were some individuals who commanded universal respect. Perhaps the greatest of these was Dauda Kwoi. With the Chief of Kagoro, another leader of great merit, he guided the aspirations of his people with wisdom and restraint. His influence extended far beyond the division. With his death in 1957 from tuberculosis the focus of the Middle Belt movement tended to shift south into Plateau Province and finally to Benue, where for a time it became essentially a Tiv affair.

But much of the initial drive and organization came from southern Zaria, based on the fears of the pagan people, beginning to benefit from Western education, of the Moslem Fulani-Hausa overlordship of Zaria. The Minorities Commission recognized these fears[15] but considered that unity could have the same effect as separation in remedying them. "In a few years time, a Nigeria which has to face the outer world may find within herself forces working strongly for unity. It would be a pity if, at the moment when Nigeria achieved independence, separate states had been created which enshrined tribal separation in a political form which was designed to be permanent."[16]

The commission recommended various constitutional safeguards for minorities and for a while these seemed to work well. The NPC's Northernization Policy as well which emphasized the slogan "One North, One People," gave a considerable boost to Middle Belt aspirations in employment. But the early promise was short lived. As the years went by the political elite became entrenched in its enjoyment of power, and "the decline in consti-

15. *Minorities Commission Report,* p. 72.
16. *Ibid.,* p. 88.

tutionalism through falsified censuses and rigged elections and the failure to work out 'the rules of the game,' led to a situation in which 'clubs became trumps.' "[17]

Not only were the constitutional safeguards of little real value, but the prospect of religious conflict between Moslem and Christian, always latent but for long quiescent due to an unusually high degree of mutual tolerance, became more serious as in the last two years of his life the Sardauna of Sokoto became actively involved in militant proselytization of Islam.

The Middle Belt political parties were virtually dead in 1965, except for the open rebellion of the Tiv people, but the Northern Christian Association was becoming an effective and important lobby, the more so because it did not rely in any way upon expatriate missionaries. Although the association was primarily concerned with problems arising from too ardent a support of the Sardauna's Islamic missionary enterprise by some provincial commissioners, NA's, and district and village heads, much of its strength came from educated Middle Belters who resented what they felt to be a position of inferiority as, to use their phrase, "counterfeit Northerners."

The effect of prolonged exposure to Western education brought by the missionaries was making itself felt. The same problem of educational imbalance which caused tension between the North and South of Nigeria had arisen within the North itself, between the "true," "holy," "dry," "respectable" (all adjectives in common use by British officials) North and the Middle Belt. Just as the efforts to integrate southern Zaria by giving it some measure of self-government went by the board after the British withdrawal, so too in the region no effort was made to implement the Hudson proposals for provincial governments after the retirement of Sir Bryan Sharwood Smith, the last effective British governor and imaginative author of the "twelve pillars policy."[18] At the time of writing it is increasingly clear that some form of decentralization will be essential if Nigeria is to survive.

17. James O'Connell, "Political Integration. The Nigerian Case," in *African Integration and Disintegration,* ed. A. Hazlewood (London: Oxford University Press, 1967), p. 172.
18. R. S. Hudson, *Provincial Authorities* (Kaduna: Government Printer, 1957).

Then, of course, those of us working in Middle Belt areas did not quite see it in this way. We were affronted by obvious injustice, shamed by the failures of our pagan protégés, and anxious somehow or other to provide a peaceful compromise. Most of us had some sympathy with both sides. I wanted the Fulani Empire to accept that it too, like the British, had to come to terms with its subject peoples and would be better off in the long run if it did so graciously and justly.

Nobody, I think, realized then how fast would be the change in southern Zaria. It stands in a key position, midway between the Hausa-Fulani states and the big obviously Middle Belt peoples such as the Tiv, Idoma, Igala, and Yoruba. It was still achieving internal unity, helped by the Hausa language and NA system as well as by common Christian conviction and education. Progress has been as spectacular as that of the Ibo in Eastern Nigeria, although beginning some thirty years later. It is one of the most dynamic and exciting areas of Nigeria and its people have a great future.

✻

My finance schedule gave me plenty to do apart from promoting the welfare of southern Zaria. I supervised the NA finances, without, however, having direct control. It could be irritating. In theory the treasury staff were supposed to keep all the books, handle the cash, prepare estimates and accounts. In practice one had to do a great deal of the detailed work one's self, particularly the preparation of the monthly balance sheet. I not only drafted the 1955/56 estimates but actually typed them myself. It was not that the treasury staff were completely incompetent, they just did not see the need to worry about such formalities. Senior NA officials, from the emir down, would only complain when their salaries or allowances failed to turn up on time. If they ever thought about it at all, they were probably in favor of not having certain accounts too well kept. We were the ones who worried and who received the kicks from headquarters. Never any use at figures, I accepted the tiresome side of the job because of the opportunities it gave me to ease money out of the treasury to the districts. People who keep accounts inefficiently often don't know where all the funds are. I discovered some useful votes of approved expenditure, long since forgotten but with healthy balances. I quickly applied some of these balances to favorite projects which were held up for lack of money.

The city of Zaria, itself a district in the emirate structure, was also the preserve of the ADO in charge of finance. I sometimes stayed there and would stroll around the streets in the evening. There were some worthwhile young men in the NA. Two brothers, sons of the district head of the city, himself an able man, were later to be my students at the Institute of Administration and ultimately colleagues. Together we built a playing field within the city walls and the ADO's presented a challenge cup for the city football league which one of the brothers was promoting. Soccer was still mainly confined to Southerners and the *sabon gari*. City elders were shocked at the thought of their youngsters playing football. The game could be tolerated among junior primary schoolchildren, but once past puberty a young man was expected to settle down and give up childish pastimes. I had a trump card however. The city branch of NEPU, the opposition party, was very active. There were meetings nearly every evening. These attracted not only members and potential supporters but every idle youth and child in the town. Just before our first football match I took the District Head on an evening drive, taking care to pass the NEPU meeting. I pointed out to him the size of the crowd. On the day of the match, with the army fifes and drums to play in the interval as an added attraction, I pulled away the District Head before the end. We drove off to the NEPU meeting place. An ardent politician was addressing the thinnest crowd of his experience, and there was not a youth or child to be seen. They were all at the match.

❀

The central administration of the NA was overlooked by the *Waziri*, a delightful old man of wizened stature, sly humor, and shrewd wisdom. I saw him daily. Although blinded through unwise acceptance of arsenical injections from a dispenser relative, the old man refused to give up his job. He would be warned of my arrival by a messenger and, in one movement worthy of a ballet dancer, his long-fingered slender right hand slid kola nut from his mouth into a spitoon, retrieved dentures from the same unsavory receptacle, inserted them, and passed on to clasp my own in greeting as I approached his left side. I knew that he would always keep me engaged in conversation until the clock chimed. Then, a few moments having passed, he would gaze intently at the space on the wall where hung the clock and announce that it was five minutes past the hour which had just struck to prove that he was not as blind as we knew him to be.

The *Waziri* was a master of the Fulani art of agreeing and then either doing nothing or acting in the reverse manner to that agreed. Examining the NA personal emoluments register one day I discovered a dozen or so messengers on the payroll for whom there was no authorized establishment. As the establishment of messengers was already higher than could reasonably be justified and the treasury was on the brink of unsoundness, I could not hope to make out a case for further unproductive expenditure. I arranged with the *Waziri* to parade the entire corps of messengers. A great array of the halt, the lame, and the blind, most of them very aged, assembled. We were all somewhat surprised at who turned up. Some of them had certainly never carried a message in my time.

I suggested to the *Waziri* how sad it was that the elderly and infirm had not been able to lay down the burden of office and enjoy a well-earned rest. I worked out the retirement benefits for each of them and proposed that the oldest and longest in service be retired on grounds of age and the establishment put back to rights accordingly.

The *Waziri* agreed. I was delighted with my stratagem. I had proof that my philosophy of positive administration worked. Had I just nagged at the NA about the unauthorized overestablishment or demanded dismissal of unauthorized staff there would have been bitter opposition and at best the dismissal of the newest, youngest, and probably most useful messengers. By emphasizing the retirement benefits aspect I had achieved my purpose with general satisfaction all around.

But I had counted my victory too soon. A few weeks later I was once again checking the personal emoluments register. To my surprise and annoyance I found that from the month the old men had been retired and gone onto the pension list each one of them had been replaced. A member of the Appointments Committee, I knew that no such appointments had been authorized according to the rules. I went to the *Waziri*. When old men are retired because they are too feeble to work, he explained, it was only just that their sons should support them. Even Christians he thought would support this divine injunction. I had to admit that it was good to support one's aged parents. Well then, he said, "I have given in each case the father's job to one of his sons. Is this not good and just?"

His finest outwittal of the British bureaucracy was over his first motorcar. Buying it with an advance of salary, he allowed a mechanically inexperienced relative to be his driver. Rough roads loosened the sump plug, oil leaked and was not replenished. In a few weeks the car lay idle with a seized-up engine. Replacements were not available, neither was it possible in Zaria to regrind the crankshaft. The *Waziri* told the treasury to stop making deductions from his salary. When eventually an audit query forced pressure the old man, renowned and respected for his Koranic learning, brought forth arguments carefully based on the Prophet's strictures to prove that it would be immoral for him to pay for a car he could not use. The Financial Secretary was welcome to the car which was all but new if he wanted it. After a few months of argument that august person gave up the battle, and the *Waziri* purchased another car on another advance.

*

Although he remained in the background the Emir, Ja'afaru, held the reins of power tightly. Once a week, usually on Sunday morning, the council met. As neither Resident nor SDO enjoyed disturbing their Sabbath rest a junior officer, sometimes myself, was usually detailed to attend. The Emir treated me like a rather difficult grandson. The council accepted whatever he said with a chorus of "Ran Sarki ya dade,"[19] much as I, when a private soldier,

19. The Hausa term of respectful address to an emir, meaning literally "Long live the king."

replied "Sir" to every command. The Emir held all the initiative.

This chant of yes men plagued all British administrators and most of those who have written about their work make comment. For a long while the House of Chiefs, the upper house of Northern Nigeria's legislature, was known to expatriates as the "Hakanunnery," a play on the Hausa word *hakannan* meaning "so be it." The witty expatriate Attorney-General once remarked that the House must be the only major legislative body in the world which conducted the majority of its business in silence!

I sat beside the Emir at these Sunday morning NA council meetings. There was no table. The councilors were seated down the sides of the room, leaving space on the floor in the center for an occasional official summoned into the chamber to be given instructions. Barefooted, he would prostrate himself before the Emir and mumble "Ran Sarki ya dade" whenever the Emir paused. From time to time during council deliberations the Emir would turn to me and say, "DO, you hear what they say?" I would then be given my instructions. I hated being exposed to the Emir's interpretation of indirect rule, but it was not his fault. I must have seemed like an obnoxious insect buzzing in his ear.

Later on, after the death of Ja'afaru, the Zaria palace was made something of a showpiece, largely through the efforts of the administration. But in my day it was a dismal place. The usual audience chamber was a dark and dirty hall. The Emir sat in a large chair hidden with innumerable dusty velvet coverings. Visitors sat on the more hideous and uncomfortable type of metal stacking chair. By the Emir's side was a table, covered with a cheap and gaudy blanket, on which stood incongruously a dusty calendar advertising Johnny Walker whisky. On special occasions visitors were received in the residential part of the palace. I remember when the Secretary of State for the Colonies was due being sent by the Resident on the delicate errand of making sure that the room was presentable. "And try if you can, Smith, to get the bed moved out, or at least hidden by a curtain."

Like a good many administrative officers in Zaria I eventually fell foul of the Emir, but in the end we parted as friends. However angry I might be I was always overcome by his dignified charm and the respect I felt for his age and experience. I couldn't help but like him and always wished that I could avoid exposure to conflict. He blamed the British for most of his worries and in particular for politics and the unwise promotion of democratic ideas. Sir Hugh Foot, who as chief secretary had initiated much of the political reform, was the Emir's special dislike. The senior administrative staff in Zaria tended to agree with the old man. They all referred to political developments candidly enough as "foot rot."

My clash with the Emir came in curious circumstances. The sudden announcement toward the end of 1955 of a visit to Nigeria by the Queen stole from Zaria the Resident and a sparkling new SDO in whom all we youngsters had great hopes. Like many of his kind he spent most of his career bottled up in headquarters to the detriment of the provinces. An officer who had been intriguing for a dry northern posting after a long term in the Middle Belt arrived as acting resident. I was left in charge of the division until a more senior man returned from leave.

Just about this time the Emir had pointed out that he had only one saloon car. This was his own vehicle, purchased with an advance from the House of Chiefs of which he was an ex officio member and from which he drew a legislator's salary and allowances. Most emirs, and certainly his colleagues in the Executive Council, for he was a minister without portfolio too, had at least one official car provided by their native authorities. He too wanted an NA car. His request seemed very reasonable to me. Apart from anything else his present car was four years old.

Unfortunately decision of this sort involved much red tape before implementation. The approved budget for the year contained no provision for expenditure on a car. Capital expenditure had, moreover, to be written into a five-year development plan. The Zaria plan's provision for replacement of NA vehicles was already fully committed. Juggling with figures and approval of the Financial Secretary was needed. I did all the spadework for the NA, building up small surpluses from completed projects to find the necessary funds. I drafted a suitable letter, seeking approval and strongly recommending it, for the Resident to sign. At least six weeks would be needed before an answer came through, and I was far too unimportant to do any effective worrying by telephone.

The old man began to fuss me daily. To keep him happy I suggested that he decide on the type of car he wanted so that I could arrange for the import license necessary for a dollar-imported vehicle and place the order. He told me that all he wanted was the cash. There was no need for me to worry about anything else. Inquiry told me what I ought to have known from the start. The Emir proposed selling his own car—four years old, purchased on a government advance, and earning a handsome basic and mileage allowance—to the NA for the price of a new car. The mechanical engineer valued the car at about a fifth of the sum which had now been approved and written into the budget. I stalled for time and told the acting Resident that I thought it was too big for me to handle. The Emir was not only a first class chief but a minister without portfolio. I was still that humblest of administrative bottle-washers—an ADO.

A few days later at a council meeting, with both acting Resident and myself present, the Emir, other business having been discussed, inquired why he still had not received the money for his car. Approval had arrived, but by delaying it in the provincial office I had prevented the treasury from making out a check. I looked hopefully to my senior, although I pitied him the difficult task. He looked at his watch, jumped up and excused himself on the pretext of an appointment. "The DO will explain about the car." The Emir never forgave me for what I then had to say even though in the end he got his money and the NA took over the car. He even continued to draw allowances on it from the legislature.

As in so many other financial matters it was all but impossible for us in the provinces to force the strict implementation of the government regulations for the handling of NA funds when an important chief was involved. The advent of politics and participation in the regional government by such chiefs made it even more difficult. It became embarrassing to inspect too closely a wide variety of accounts. Audit would press queries through the provincial administration and the Financial Secretary would cajole and criticize. But what could one do about personal advances, for example, when these were too many? The largest and longest outstanding would be against the emir. If he could not be pursued, what hope was there of enlisting his support in chasing less important officials? We confined ourselves to pressing for the repayment of the £15 advances to humble police constables and their like for the purchase of a cycle. The mighty, unless out of favor at court, went untouched.

This was one of the weaknesses of the British position immediately prior to independence. To avoid accusations of racial prejudice and imperialistic deceit we more or less sat back and watched the elite, to whom in practice we were going to hand over the power, build up for themselves an unassailable position of privilege. When eventually the day of reckoning came it was bloody and prolonged. Years of hard work were lost. The rule of law was thrown aside and standards of conduct barely achieved were lost again. I wonder whether greater firmness in the early political days might have been of better service to Nigeria in the long run. If only it were easy to be both liberal and tough!

The Emir soon had an opportunity to express his disapproval of me. When the Premier paid a visit to Zaria I met him for the first time. The Northern Premier was an outstanding man by any measure. His big stature was matched by a personality which readily dominated any group he was with. His noble blood undoubtedly helped the Sardauna of Sokoto achieve his political prominence, but there was much more to it than this. In capacity he stood head and shoulders above his contemporaries. By 1955 his leadership of the Northern Peoples' Congress was secure and he was daily becoming more and more of a power in the land.

At the council meeting held in his honor I sat at the end of the row of visiting dignitaries. The usual exchanges of flattery took place. Then, just as I thought we were through, one of the council said he had a matter to raise. This surprised me. In two years I had never known a council member to take the initiative. For several minutes he sang the praises of the Premier. He went on to say how well things were in Zaria and how happy everyone was with the government. There was, however, one problem. A particular person managed to spoil their happiness and retard progress. My heart beat, was this to be an attack on the Emir? Any political business with the Premier, I was sure, would be conducted in private. Councils had been known to turn against their chief, and they would naturally prefer to make the attack in the restraining presence of British officials. How naïve I was!

Once the councilor had blurted out the words "DO," the Emir took over. "This boy refuses to allow me to do as I like in *my* treasury," and so on. The Premier calmly quelled the attack but looked to the acting Resident for an explanation. None of us had ever done more than try and have *Financial Memoranda,* the government rules for running a treasury, followed at least half-heartedly. I was prepared to be a scapegoat but not, as happened, to be thrown trussed and gutted to the wolves. The acting Resident said how distressed he was to hear the complaint and why had the Emir not spoken to him before. He would at once look into the matter. The Emir turned to me and said: "DO, do you hear?" "To, na ji,"[20] I replied in a voice red hot with anger.

I cursed many people that day, including the unfortunate Queen, whose pending visit had thrust me into the situation in the first place. When fellow ADO's gathered in the evening to hear an account of the day, my letter of resignation was written. But after a drink or two I was laughing it off, my spirits restored by the good sense and friendship of my colleagues. It was also my good fortune that the Premier's Secretary happened to be the SDO so rudely removed from the division. He wrote me the kindest of letters and assured me he not only understood but had done his best to explain to the Premier. It was four years later, after I had been working a few weeks in his own office, that the Premier let me know, in one of those characteristically kind moments of his, that my name had been crossed from the black list. The action of the Premier's Secretary was as typical of the service as that of my acting Resident was not.

*

The prison was one of the interests of the ADO with the finance schedule. Every Tuesday morning, dressed in jacket and long

20. "Yes, I hear!"

trousers, I inspected prison, prisoners, and warders before breakfast. The daily lockup averaged four hundred. The main prison
was surrounded by a huge mud wall and still contained several
ancient mud cells. A smaller prison was located on the outskirts of
the township where the expatriates lived. Nigerian prisons are on
the whole friendly places. I have always hoped that if fate should
ever direct my imprisonment that it be in Nigeria rather than in
England. But the Zaria prison had a bad record and discipline
was still bad. One prisoner, an ex-policeman and a stranger,
terrorized the prison during my time. I arranged for his transfer
to a tougher, government prison. Regulations decreed that he first
be medically examined. He refused to submit to the examination.
It was a Sunday morning, the only time in the week the busy
doctor had to give to the prison. I got a lorry and a riot unit of
police to stand by. The troublesome prisoner refused to listen to
me and the warders were afraid to touch him. I did not want him
to add assault to his other crimes, so, after we had managed to
lock up the other prisoners, I moved in the riot squad and he gave
up. Apart from a knife, he possessed a large sum of money. Once
he had gone I searched the prison thoroughly and we produced a
handsome cache of weapons of one sort or another.

The prisoners seemed glad to see the end of their strong man,
and I took the opportunity to embark on a policy of separating
young and first offenders from the recidivists, making use of the
two prisons. I also pushed warder training and got them, the
lowest paid and most neglected NA servants, improved salaries
and better uniforms. A colleague who succeeded me carried on
this interest, and eventually the prison reached a high standard.

Capital cases gave me the most personal anxiety. I had long
been in favor of the abolition of capital punishment. Working
with and on behalf of condemned prisoners forcefully confirmed
my beliefs. Executions, thank God, were no longer carried out in
NA prisons, but it was my lot to tell a prisoner that all his appeals
had failed, that the warrant of execution was signed, and send
him off to his death at Kaduna. Nothing has ever given me greater
satisfaction than the news that a murderer, whom I had grown to
like well over many months of appeals to higher courts, had had
his sentence commuted to one of life imprisonment. I had myself

drafted his letter of petition to the Governor asking for the exercise of the prerogative of mercy. He was a simple peasant who had killed his mother-in-law under great provocation, never intending to strike as hard as he did.

For such people the British courts were impossible to understand, with their ritual and fancy dress, and curious approach to truth. They invariably confessed their guilt and told the factual story of what happened. The subtleties of pleading not guilty before the law and only answering the exact questions put to them were too much.

In many ways the local courts were vastly superior, however much more open to corruption. I have never been impressed anywhere that justice was being done so much as in a simple pagan court in southern Zaria. It met in a courthouse half open to the elements. The elders of the tribe, court members, acted as judges, jury, counsel for the prosecution, counsel for the defense, and witnesses as the occasion demanded and the mood took them. The court was open and anyone present was permitted to comment. The truth was always found out, and justice acceptable to the majority applied. Appeals from such courts were as rare as diamonds.

The notion that native courts, as they were known, were a bad thing grew up largely from the fact that lawyers were not permitted to practice in them. Recruitment policy of the unified British Colonial Service, which in theory served all colonial territories, for long made it difficult for an educated Nigerian to obtain a senior appointment in the public service. The law offered an alternative and the bar exams were at that time perhaps the easiest and cheapest way to a graduate type qualification. Inevitably a legal profession brimming over with new members cast an envious eye on the native courts in which 80 per cent of all litigation was heard. A barrister in a southern Zaria court such as I have described would have produced a situation as comical as it would have been chaotic.

As time went on, however, there was much to be said for replacing the native courts in the urban areas with more professional courts in which lawyers could practice. A cosmopolitan urban community could not reproduce the ideal conditions for native courts. Corruption and political interference became more and more common and ultimate criticism of these courts was to a large extent justified. Where outside observers were so often wrong were the way in which they naïvely presumed that magistrates' courts were free of corruption, and the manner in which they talked of political prisoners. I never came across such a prisoner. If I had in my weekly inspections found a man in prison without a warrant stating his offense, the law involved, and the court which imposed the sentence, I would have released him. What in fact happened was this. The party in power represented the establishment, and native courts were part of the establishment. When political heat was generated above a certain temperature civil authorities, police, and courts all became unusually assiduous in applying the law. But they applied it in the main against political opponents. It was not difficult. One of the things likely to attract a man to the opposition party was his general irritation with authority and often negligent citizenship. He probably was a tax defaulter, or minor lawbreaker in some way or another. Before the introduction of the Penal Code there were also offenses under native law and custom which looked pretty curious to a Western eye—refusing the order of a chief, for example. But for the most part the so-called political prisoners were picked up for tax defaulting, holding meetings without permits, and in Moslem areas for drinking, or breaking the fast, both offenses under Maliki law.

Experience in prisons confirmed me in my views in favor of abolition of capital punishment but reversed my preconceived notions about corporal punishment, at least as far as Nigerian prisoners were concerned. There was, of course, the danger of the punishment's being carried out sadistically, but I only once came across such a case. Usually the prison warder assigned to the task was an elderly and avuncular character without an ounce of malice in him. It always seemed to me much better that first offenders should be beaten and kept out of contact with prisoners. It was in many ways a better deterrent, there being little stigma attached to prison sentences but some fear of corporal punishment. Nobody wanted to spend much money on prisons when there was so much to be done to develop other social services, so it would be many years before a sophisticated prison system could safely look after first and juvenile offenders and discharge them rehabilitated rather than worsened by contact with experienced criminals.

If the prison gave me food for thought, it also provided amusement. On Tuesday mornings I first inspected the parade of warders. Then we moved farther into the prison and the prisoners were paraded in the yard. The Chief Warder, a retired sergeant-major, had a wonderful parade ground voice worthy of the guards depot. As I came into the yard he would about turn to face me and give me a magnificent salute. He then reeled off the day's state of prisoner and warder strength. His memory was as weak as his voice was strong. Tens, hundreds, and thousands were apt to get muddled despite the *aide-mémoire* he inscribed on the palm of his left hand with a ball-point pen. I then proceeded to inspect the ranks of prisoners. Week after week his bellow of "Parade—shun!" produced never a movement as row upon row of stolid peasants and urban rascals watched the performance, many with a twinkle in the eye.

Twice the prison gave me amusement which was more obvious in retrospect than at the time. A plane carrying the Director of Prisons as a passenger made a forced landing at Zaria one afternoon. As the necessary repairs were going to take a couple of hours the Director, one of the modern school of humane and intelligent prison governors, decided to take a look at the prison. I rose from a siesta to escort him. The city telephone exchange was off duty. We arrived at the prison gates perforce unannounced. No warder was to be seen. The Chief Warder's house opposite the gate was bathed in rustic calm. An adult male, I could not enter uninvited. The *zaure* was empty and no small boy came conveniently by. I went back to the prison gate and shouted, hoping that some sleepy warder would emerge from the office. Instead a prisoner came to the grill. We had a rapid and conspiratorial conversation in Hausa, a language I hoped the Director of Prisons could not understand. I gathered that all the warders were at home resting. The prisoner offered to fetch them and ducking into the office came back with the keys to let us in and he out. Trying to look as though this were a perfectly normal procedure in the best of progressive prisons, I ushered in the Director. The helpful prisoner showed me the right key for the inner yard and ran off to rouse his custodians. I had almost completed the round of the cells when a few warders, hot and panting, arrived. As he signed the visitors' book the Director grinned at me and said: "I've known prisons where this happened too!"

A judge of the High Court was not so accommodating. Adjourning court one Saturday morning at a time when good officials were imbibing beer or pink gins, he informed the Resident that he wished to inspect the prison, a right of the High Court. The Resident summoned me from what was clearly going to be a very good curry lunch party. I rushed home to put on a suit and found a testy judge fuming at the delay. I tried to hurry him around, but either to get his own back or because he habitually did not eat lunch himself he took his time. He even insisted on visiting the lunatics. One old lady who had been confined for twenty years or more, committed on an arson charge, began to babble away at the Judge, as she always did to new faces. I told the sad story of her committal and of her present addiction to her past crime, on which account she could not safely be released. "What is she saying?" he demanded. Foolishly I told him, not imagining that anyone, least of all an experienced judge, would take it as more than the pathetic nonsense of a disordered mind. "She's telling you, Sir, that I am trying to poison her by tampering with her food." "Oh, is she. This is a serious charge. What else does she have to say? No, no, you are involved. Let somebody else interpret." I had then to stand by for nearly an hour while the old lady went on and on laying even wilder accusations against me and a variety of others until even the Judge tired and went back to his resthouse. I have often wondered what, if anything, he put in his report!

❈

The development of local government on democratic and representative lines reached a stage at which the city of Zaria was to have a town council with a number of devolved powers. On the whole native authorities were reluctant to delegate authority in the place where it most hurt—the headquarters of the emirate. The administrative weapon was to point out that the stranger element in the *sabon gari* would soon demand such powers and therefore it should be hastened in the native town first.

For months electoral regulations were drafted and redrafted. I played little part in this, for a senior colleague responsible for local government spent most of his time handling the legal aspects. When, however, all was drafted and approved and ready for the first election the NA appointed me as the electoral officer. No pressure was put upon them to do so. It was generally accepted that elections meant a lot of work, and the fussy sort of work best performed by an administrative officer. It was also believed that the populace respected an election conducted by an expatriate—in practice in 1955 they had seen little else. I was the ADO most involved in the city administration and best known to the people, hence my selection.

Apart from arranging for the conduct of the election, which was simple enough, I determined to educate the public. Each election, whether national or local, tended to be more progressive than the last as far as procedures were concerned. With each electoral experience we hoped that the ordinary people would gain in their understanding of the representative principle in government. Evening after evening I toured the city and addressed public meetings on the electoral procedure and the future role of the council once elected. In this I was accompanied by the district head, the *Sarkin Fada*.

The party in power in the region, the NPC, was poorly organized in Zaria and very passive. NEPU, the opposition in the Hausa areas, however, was very active about this time. The election gave the party leaders something to do other than sponsor complainants. The party held many meetings to urge the voters to support the NEPU cause. Most of what was said was of the rabble-rousing negative polemics common to hustings. The innumerable children of the city loved it. They had little else to do. As NEPU held meetings and as I held meetings, both about elections, the children lumped us together. My car was daily pursued along the narrow and rutted city streets by a horde of ragamuffins, chanting "baturen Nefu, baturen Nefu"—"The NEPU white man." Luckily I was able to get the district head to clear me when traditionalists in the council took it for granted that I was urging everyone to vote for NEPU. I was lucky too that at this time the province had both an excellent and understanding resident and SDO, both of whom accompanied me to one of my meetings.

As the election drew closer it was clear that NEPU knew what it was about. Party officials sought several interviews to clarify procedural issues. Voting was by wards and each ward was a multimember constituency. Such constituencies were a common and bad mistake in our early attempts at representative government but often a necessary compromise because of the difficulties of cutting up traditional areas of authority, thus creating all sorts of suspicions and status problems. Zaria had five wards, four in the city and one outside at Tudun Wada, a stranger settlement. They were too large to return only one member. Yet there was no way to split them without the danger of the man elected assuming an authority for a geographical unit which was not rightfully his. This tendency for elected representatives to don the mantle of aristocracy has been common to the African scene and has since independence contributed to the downfall of parliamentary system after parliamentary system.

NEPU understood the problem and knew that multimember constituencies necessitated strong party discipline. They sorted out their candidates in good time. They nominated the exact number required for each constituency. The NPC, on the other hand, found it difficult to do this—whether from aristocratic inertia, lack of political experience, or simple pride is hard to say. I several times suggested to the local party leader, Nuhu Bamalli, that he try and get the party's candidates sorted out beforehand. He more or less told me to mind my own business. I foresaw a NEPU victory because the NA was unpopular in the city, but I felt it would be better for all concerned, including myself, if the election could be won in an obvious way and not be complicated by split votes. In the event, in the ward of the city where lived the important families and in which stood the palace, there were eighty-six NPC candidates for six seats. A similar situation, although on a lesser scale, prevailed elsewhere.

The "whispered vote" system of ballot was written into the regulations. This meant that the polling officer had to read, in this one ward, to every one of the voters as they came by turn into the polling station the names of eighty-six NPC candidates and six NEPU candidates, and then ask for which six the voter wished to vote. The unfortunate education officer who had landed this job was stuck in the polling station from 8 A.M. to 6 P.M. for two days.

NEPU, needless to say, won with a large majority. They would have won in any case, for the mid-fifties was the time when the establishment was least popular in the North as witnessed by the regional elections of 1956. But the split voting of the NPC handed them everything.

I spent the whole of the election days—we had to spend two days because of the number of candidates—moving around the polling stations keeping an eye on things. Voters turned out in good numbers. It was a very warm day in the "little" hot season of October. NEPU produced umbrellas, painted with slogans, to shield their supporters from the sun as they queued to vote. There was plenty of good-humored ribaldry but I saw no jostling.

After the election the NPC filed the inevitable objections, stating that the conduct of the election was unfair and that NPC supporters were prevented from voting by NEPU thugs. Certainly many respectable citizens objected to lining up. They expected precedence in voting as in other things in life. It was to take a disastrous regional election in Zaria the following year before the NPC began to learn political sense and persuade its followers that the success of a democratic election depended upon organization, discipline, and effort as well as Allah.

Some years later I saw my report on the elections which had been sent to Kaduna. Against my comments and evidence of fair conduct the Premier's green ink recorded "Allah dai, ya sani!"— "God knows the truth!" As the British withdrew so the opposition parties shrank away. The concept of a parliamentary opposition was perhaps the most difficult pill to swallow in the Westminster bottle. It was a concept understood by neither side. The opposition was as irresponsible and foolish in its behavior as the party in power was petty and vindictive in its actions against it. Political opposition could thrive while the British held the ring. When the colonial referee was no longer present the opposition was soon counted out, more often by the bribe of office than by thuggery. The safety valves of democratic government were closed and the ultimate explosion was violent. An interesting yardstick is the debates in the Northern House of Assembly. Before independence these could be lively and worthwhile. A budget session seemed to matter. After self-government sessions became shorter and shorter until toward the end little of moment was said at all. In August, 1962, the House reached a record peak of performance when it considered fourteen bills through their stages in a one-day sitting with hardly a speech made.

✱

My fondness of the bush prevented me from sitting week in, week out in Zaria. My schedule offered no touring, but I decided that in order to keep sane I must at least once a month get out and taste the flavor of the districts again. It suited colleagues well that I adopt a particular district, so I used to spend weekends and sometimes a public holiday at Kajuru, an interesting district some ninety miles south of Zaria on good roads. Like Kauru it was a former Habe vassal state, but whereas the pagan people of Kauru were many and varied and there was a substantial Hausa element in the district, the only Hausa in Kajuru were a handful in the headquarters and the mass of people were all of one pagan tribe, the Kadara.

Kajuru was delightfully situated amid rocky hills. There was a rather delapidated mud resthouse. I decided to get funds out of Kaduna for a permanent replacement. I thought that if ever I were unfortunate enough to be posted to a ministry I would like to have a funk hole in the bush a mere forty miles away. I pleaded the usual arguments of administrative convenience and suggested use of a good resthouse as a recreational facility for hard-worked secretariat officers. I lied that the existing structure had fallen down. The letter requesting funds arrived on the desk of the appropriate officer in the Financial Secretary's Office on a Monday morning. He was a keen hunter and had spent the weekend on a shooting trip at Kajuru resthouse. My argument about recreational facilities appealed, he connived in my lie, and the funds arrived with unusual dispatch.

The administration and the Public Works Department were never the best of friends. So much good could have been done by the right kind of engineer, but somehow or other they always seemed to get bogged down in pettifogging administration and rare indeed was the man who would do anything at all to help a native authority. There was nothing of the aura of indirect rule about their department, although government quite unfairly made native authorities finance, without any return of interest, huge government roads and buildings projects on advance accounts. So a lot of the fun the young engineers might have got out of their job, if only they had tried, came our way. We all enjoyed building and road-making, in small doses at least. The professionals usually sneered at our efforts but made good use of them, and to this day many of the best road lines in Nigeria were traced by a DO in his spare time.

The Provincial Engineer, as I expected, was not going to waste his time on designing a resthouse. All the better, I was able to do it myself and incorporate the features I considered most important. As a consumer I was probably much better qualified than any engineer, few of whom left the comfort of their houses for more than a day at a time. So I designed the resthouse, with a huge veranda surrounded by a wall on which one could sit in comfort, and let the contract. The work was completed about the time of the Queen's visit. I was away in Kaduna with the Durbar contingent when the contractor came to report. I received a charming letter from him in which he explained how "he had found me absent" and had traveled to Kaduna where he had visited every hotel in town but failed to find the Dur Bar!

The district council at Kajuru was a special pleasure. It was lively and the district head displayed great skill and tact in handling an alien people, traditionally his subjects, sharply divided due to mission influence on the young. Representatives from villages where missions had not penetrated were old men. They invariably clashed with the young hotheaded semiliterates elected in mission-influenced villages.

It was the custom for Kadara girls to wear nothing except a simple covering of colored beads. After marriage and pregnancy the women went completely nude. The men wore only loincloths, and the youths affected beads and a skin to sit upon. Mission adherents, however, wore Hausa dress. They were mainly youths and boys, very few women having adopted Christianity. At one council meeting the mission faction proposed that nudity be banned by legislation. They argued, as might be expected, of shame before other people and sexual misdemeanors. The old men were not impressed. The Kadara had a very strict and well-kept code of sexual ethics which only the young mission men were breaking. The only clothed women the men knew were the lower-class Hausa women of Kajuru who were not in purdah and an occasional prostitute migrating southward. Neither were renowned for strict morality. The chief, a Moslem and therefore offended by nudity, kept the balance beautifully, assuring the young that time was on their side, they had but to be patient a little longer, and letting the old know that he would not allow the council to upset traditions still honored by the majority.

The council voted money for a footbridge and drift over the stream between the town and main road. The funds were used for cement and a mason. The rest of the work we did with community labor. Perhaps because they were surrounded by virile and lively pagans the Kajuru Hausa seemed to have more go and zest than the average Hausa community. We only worked at weekends when I could be present. Everyone turned out, including the chief. It was enormous fun and in no time we had the footbridge built. I made friends I was to know for years afterward. The bridge, alas, was burned down one dry season, and no effort ever made to replace it, but the concrete drift keeps the road open all the year except after very high floods. But give me a week or two in Kajuru and I believe the footbridge would soon be up again. The chief is no more and his successor lacks his authority, but the people have a good spirit.

One of the saddest things in Northern Nigeria, and no doubt it is true of many parts of Africa, is to see how little the people help themselves in matters well within the technical competence of the community. It is often hard for a member of the community to exert the same leadership as an outsider. He speedily arouses hostility from traditional leadership, a rival family, or his own age group competitors. Where a traditional leader is firmly seated and is prepared also to play the role of modernization leader, development can be rapid and marked. Kagoro, under the chieftaincy of Gwamna, in southern Zaria is an example of such a situation. Had *Sarkin Kajuru* had strong support from an ADO and felt more at ease with Zaria NA perhaps he might have achieved more.

Together we once went to look into a border dispute between a Kadara village in Kajuru District and a Gwari village in Chikum District. A considerable acreage of newly opened farmland was involved and the district heads were as interested as the villagers themselves. Historically it was clear that both parties had moved into the land in recent times and that, despite their claims, it was a comparatively new dispute and not, like so many, with roots in the distant past and a future stretching into eternity. With the district head of Chikum we listened patiently to each side and then went to view the ground. There was a stream flowing through the center of it in the right direction; no geographer could have plotted a better boundary. I hopefully suggested the obvious administrative compromise. It was vigorously rejected by both parties. I had learned from experience and the wisdom of my seniors that outsiders never *settle* boundary disputes. They can, however, fill the useful role of impartial witnesses to an agreement between the opposing sides. I announced that I would remain until the Kadara and Gwari worked out a solution for themselves, staying in each village on alternate nights, and proposed we all meet on the site the following day.

Next day after a long wait the Kadara eventually offered to

accept the Gwari claim in full on condition that the Gwari chief swore on the Kadara oath that his claim was lawful. I inquired privately what would happen if the Gwari chief perjured himself. "He will die," came the calm reply. I had slept the night in the Gwari village and knew that the rather elderly chief had risen from a bed of sickness to accompany us. I was apprehensive but allowed the Gwari to accept or reject the challenge. They accepted. We all moved to the boundary line the Gwari claimed, well in among some Kadara farms. The Kadara then instructed the Gwari chief in taking the oath. He was first taken away alone to the stream where ablutions were performed. I was very glad to see him return. The rest of the oath-taking ceremony was somewhat gymnastic as the chief was required to sit on a small clay pot juju and face various directions in turn. He was also required to remove his cloth trousers, presumably because the Kadara did not wear cloth over their buttocks but an animal skin. My Moslem messenger and the emir's representative very nearly had a fit of hysterics at this point and I had to tell them to take a walk. Finally the chief was told to carry the juju and place it on what he claimed as the boundary. He stood up, perspiration streaming from every pore in his body. His face was gray and he stumbled. One of his retinue ran forward to help him. In a flash every Kadara had an arrow in his bow, strings taut and ready to be released. I called out, "Don't touch him," the retainer stopped just in time, the chief recovered from his fall and carried the ju-ju to the boundary line. He lived, and I never heard of that dispute again.

My visits to Kajuru over the years have allowed me to watch an interesting piece of rural development. When I first went, the road south of Kaduna, although a good line, was usable only in the dry season. There was little if any traffic. A leprosy clinic was set up at a point on the road where a path led in from two largish Kadara villages. A mission doctor drove or bicycled there every Thursday to administer the treatment the drug dapsone now made possible. The people who gathered for the clinic came from several areas, and soon a small food market developed. Others besides lepers came along. Then a group of young men in Kalla and Rimau decided to build a road from their villages to the main road. Meanwhile the government began to upgrade the road. The engineer in charge chose the corner with the clinic as a site for a labor camp. The Thursday clinic expanded into a substantial market. It did more than feed the road laborers, for the roadmen had transport returning empty to the farmless and hungry town of Kaduna. They bought produce to sell there, and when they moved on traders replaced them. Some people in the neighborhood decided to settle there permanently, and today there is a flourishing community with a substantial weekly market established on a busy highroad. The origin of the village is preserved in its name, Kasuwan Magani—the medicine market.

*

The visit to Nigeria in 1956 of Queen Elizabeth and the Duke of Edinburgh had greater political significance for Northern Nigeria than such imperial occasions might be expected to imply. The decision to concentrate the visit in the regional capital and bring the peoples of the North to the Queen by means of a Durbar symbolized far more effectively than had the establishment of regional executive and legislature the subordination of the provinces, and thereby the emirs and chiefs, to the regional government. The first class chiefs might have been expected to demand to entertain their sovereign in their own domains. Instead they rode at the head of their contingents to salute her on the Durbar ground, while the Premier and his ministers sat at her side. Out of the Durbar emerged a sense of unity, of "Northerness," which had never before been so obviously apparent. The Middle Belters not only felt accepted but were encouraged to come closer into the fold.

Igbirra NA at the time was an elected democratic body without a chief, the former chief having been deposed three years previously, and with him the institution of chieftaincy abolished. But after the Durbar the Igbirra notables went home convinced that the chieftaincy must be resurrected. The President of the Council told me years later of the shame they felt at alone being without a chief to greet the Queen. An elected representative could never command the same respect. They had seen too all the powerful chiefs of the region and realized how unwise it would be to continue without representation in the House of Chiefs. They proceeded to find a chief, but so concerned were they with the ceremonial aspects and the traditions of the far north that, despite Christian control of the NA, they deliberately chose a Moslem.

It was good to be alive and in the civil service at the time of the royal visit. One did not have to be either an ardent imperialist or a convinced monarchist to realize the tremendous boost the visit would give to Nigeria, on the brink of independence, in the outside world. Here too was an occasion which could guarantee both a nationalist and a political truce. With a hundred of the top pressmen of the world's greatest newspapers around we were going to hit the headlines as never before. We were all, Nigerian and expatriate, determined to give of our best. The civil service worked together with tremendous zest and energy. How often I have yearned for a similar enthusiasm since! We were given only three months in which to prepare instead of the usual year. The pressure helped and miracles were accomplished.

With his flair for identifying the right man for the job, the Governor built up a team to run the visit which could not have been excelled. Arrangements were in train in a few hours after the formal announcement. In Zaria, close to the capital, we were asked to supply all the materials for the vast camp which had to be built to accommodate seven thousand men, two thousand horses and the inevitable followers. For six weeks I rushed around the province ordering, buying, and transporting thousands upon thousands of grass mats and lengths of rope. We also had to make arrangements for the billeting and feeding of the men and horses who would pass through the province on their way to Kaduna. Some might spend three to four days trekking through the province, and some would have been on the road already for as much as forty days.

I had the good fortune and privilege to be chosen as the marshal for the provincial contingent. Our allocation was four hundred men and one hundred horses. Being so close to Kaduna it was bound to be a problem to keep numbers down, and we were, as were most provinces, well above our allocation. The numbers had to be divided between the emirate and the four independent chieftaincies. The Emir and each chief had certain retainers and musicians who would naturally be part of the contingent. The rest was made up by district heads, each being allowed fifteen men. I knew that the northerly provinces of Bornu, Kano, Sokoto, and above all Katsina with its polo-loving emir would steal the show as far as horses were concerned. The Middle Belt provinces had some good turns, the acrobatic dancers from Ilorin, the Idoma stiltmen, and so forth, but I suspected rightly that, conscious of democratic development and jealous of prestige, these provinces would tend to include all their councilors in their contingents. I resolved to persuade Zaria to concentrate on what I privately termed "circus turns." I had little difficulty. The final contingent mustered hoe dancers from Zaria, a Kadara pipe band, ju-ju dancers from Kwoi, the Emir's camel drums, and the only snakes to be included on a contingent's inventory.

As the time to move to Kaduna drew closer I visited all the districts and rehearsed each district contingent so that when finally we reached Kaduna it would be easier to fit the whole together. This was just before Christmas. My car had collapsed under the strain of so much touring and luckily I was traveling in an NA pickup. The excitement and friendliness generated by the visit was great. Nearly every district head gave me a turkey as a Christmas dash. I never felt so embarrassed at accepting gifts as when the last district head produced a turkey to stuff in with a large family of his fellows in the back of the truck. I had invitations out to every meal over the holiday and intended going out on tour again immediately afterward. I was able to present a turkey to my hostess at every engagement!

One rehearsal caused much merriment. It was in Moroa, one of the independent kingdoms of southern Zaria. The chief was fat, old, and usually drunk. He was not in the habit of riding a horse. I was accompanied to Manchok, the district headquarters, by the SDO, Zonkwa, who could be delightfully droll on occasions. The contingent was lined up, all on foot, and one rather sad-looking horse was led by a groom for the chief. The three of us sorted out the order of march and watched the group parade up and down. "Well, now, *Sarki*, what about having a ride yourself," suggested the SDO. "You never know what we may find out from a little bit of practice." The girth and unsteady hand of *Sarkin Moroa* did not facilitate mounting. More and more came to assist, unfortunately all from the one side. Eventually strength enough was mustered and the chief suddenly shot into the air, over the saddle, and onto the ground the other side! His clothing and natural upholstery prevented any serious damage, but we decided to put off any further rehearsals until the early morning when we could better guarantee his sober co-operation.

It had been agreed that the emirs and chiefs would lead their contingents past the Queen, then dismount, shake hands, and take their seats in the stand. The Emir of Zaria had not ridden a horse for years, even on the occasion of the great Moslem festivals. Tradition said that if he rode again he would die. The story had arisen after a heart attack, following which the Emir preferred not to ride. It was uncertain until the last moment whether or not Ja'afaru would be with the contingent. He attended no rehearsals, although some emirs, like the Emir of Katsina, came to the camp to ride the whole way with their people. On the morning, however, I was relieved to see the Emir drive up after we were assembled on the ground. He sat until I gave the signal, mounted, and rode after all. My problem was that he had not been rehearsed and I could not completely rely on the stand-in to be firm enough in explaining what he had to do when he reached Her Majesty. I was up at four thirty that morning and in the saddle by five. It was one thirty before we were back again in the camp. I breakfasted on the Durbar ground with my colleague from Katsina on turkey sandwiches, curry puffs, and hock.

In addition to the contingent I had a group of pagan horsemen from Piti who were to stage a mock hunt or charge at the end of the Durbar in contrast to the *jahi*[21] of the superbly dressed and mounted royal guards of the great emirates. The Piti had been difficult to get. I sent an excellent messenger, who had served me

21. Ceremonial charge of greeting.

well on many a trek, to the village with ample funds. He invited the Piti to a prolonged feast, holding it day by day closer and closer to Kaduna. Once they arrived we found it hard to keep them because they could not get the type of corn beer on which they virtually lived during the dry season. Their ponies were small hill beasts to whom the usual Northern horse seemed to take a marked objection. I was lucky to have a superb mount, the best-tempered and nicest horse to ride I ever had. The Piti, naked except for a loincloth, rode bareback and without any bridle. Their control was exercised by a single piece of cord tied around the pony's muzzle. They rode fast and fierce, hunting pig with spear. Try as we could we failed to stir up their imagination for a mock hunt on the sedate Kaduna racecourse. We were almost in despair. They could not be put in the main contingent because of the trouble their horses caused. They would have to go. We tried once more. Expatriates out for their evening stroll would gather to watch rehearsals. A lady of some distinction was exercising her dachshund. The air was full of strange and exciting smells and perhaps the little dachs fancied he sniffed a badger on the other side of the polo field. Anyway, in the best traditions of his ancestors, he charged across the vision of the Piti. With glorious shouts and a vigor we had never seen before the Piti gave chase, right into the compound of the Catering Rest House where the dachs found shelter just in time.

Well, now we knew what to do, but Her Majesty's patronage of the Royal Society for the Prevention of Cruelty to Animals urged caution. In the end we decided to let the Piti charge laterally between two of the frontal *jahi* charges. When the day came I waited with them. They had been promised they could go home to their beer as soon as it was over, provided they rode really fast. The moment drew near. First *jahi* charges from Katsina, then Kano, then Sokoto. Between Sokoto and Bornu, the final group, the Piti were to charge laterally from their place of concealment to give a surprise and extra thrill to the crowd. Even hardened press cameramen had wilted under the first charges and run helter-skelter for cover. The air was laden with dust. As the Sokoto charge reached its climax, riders stopping their horses in full gallop, rearing up under the very nose of the Queen, I ordered the Piti to get ready. The dust cleared and I saw that a Sokoto man had fallen and was lying prostrate. Nobody seemed to be going forward to collect him. I managed to restrain the Piti, thanks to the superior speed and good nature of my horse. Stretcher-bearers ran out and I gave the order to charge. Every man had his spear raised ready to throw. But the Bornu horsemen, shouting threats and calling challenges, each waving a broadsword over his head, could not be held. I foresaw a head-on collision and certain fight at the feet of the Queen and notables. I managed to stop them, but only for a few seconds, and the fleet little Piti ponies caught up with the massively furnished Bornu giants as they wheeled away from the throne. Luckily by this time both were headed in the same direction.

Being a provincial marshal at the Durbar was a grand climax to the work the preparations for the visit had entailed. The twelve of us, together with other administrative officers responsible for the camp organization, lived in the camp alongside our contingents. We had a communal mess. We worked hard and we drank hard. It was thirsty work. There was enormous merriment in the evenings. The very best of everything in the Colonial Service was apparent in those two weeks. The disappointments, the frustrations, the personal worries over future all disappeared in the wealth of good companionship, the loyalty of a well-trained team pulling together, and the sweat of hard work. It was good to be alive. Never again was the service to have an opportunity to know itself at its best, characteristically in an anonymous way as it tried to help the peoples it served show themselves to the world in the best possible light.

Epilogue

I returned to Zaria as soon as the Queen left Kaduna. I had a few financial ends to tidy but planned to go on an extended trek of Kajuru and Chikum districts within a week. I had only been back a couple of days when the Resident telephoned me and told me that the Governor wanted to see me in Kaduna. I wondered what frightful post-mortem was about to be held and where I fitted in, as witness or accused. The Resident reassured me.

On the Saturday of that week I found myself walked up and down the lawns of Government House invited to be aide-de-camp. Three days later, the day I was to have left for Kajuru, I packed up my household, said goodbye to Zaria, and drove to Kaduna. It was the end of four and a half years as cadet and ADO in the provinces. Although I had no inkling at the time, it was also virtually the end of my career in the provinces. Apart from a happy eighteen months in Kabba I was to spend the next twelve years in headquarters or training jobs of one kind or another. But to the end being a bush DO was what I liked and enjoyed most. The only regret I ever had about coming independence was the knowledge that soon there would no longer be a place for me as a district officer. It was, after all, the best job in the world. Most of my colleagues felt the same way. Some divisions were better than others, but rare was the man who, if welcoming the promotion or promise that a Residency or Secretariat posting brought, did not, at the same time, regret that his days among real people, with a freedom of action to match his heavy responsibility, were over.

Frustration may often seem to have been the theme of my narrative, but it never destroyed the excitement, the pleasures, or the sense of fulfilment which my job provided. When I was depressed it only needed a balmy night with the moon giving a magic even to the pan roofs, a comforting drink, and an understanding companion to enable me to laugh it off. Next day the first cheerful Nigerian face or glimpse of happy children at play would quickly restore my faith and renew my enthusiasm.

If I was often critical of some of my colleagues it was usually simply because their interests were not exactly mine. They, I am sure, had ample cause to be critical of me. The job, which we lived for twenty-four hours in every day and never tired of talking about, was easy on an individual's tastes. There was so much to be done that you could give full rein to your own particular interests. If you took over a division and found the courts in a mess it did not necessarily mean that your predecessor was a flop. His interests may have been roads, and perhaps these were outstanding, his particular contribution to the progress of the community. This was confusing to the Nigerians, we were all so different. It took time to assess us and judge our individual worth.

It will take time also to assess our achievement or lack of it as a service. The Colonial Service had only a short sixty years in Northern Nigeria, the first ten getting established and the last ten, the time to which I belong, paving the way for departure. The intervening forty years included two world wars and a worldwide economic depression. When the Union Jack was hauled down there were those still living who had seen it first broken. Sometimes I feel that in the years when it flew proudly over the grandeur of Government House and the mud and thatch hut of touring cadet alike, we were too few and had little enough time to leave behind us much which will long be evident. We were not only few in number, we had to leave at the very moment when the ordinary man was about ready for us. I have always wished that I could have been a touring officer in the sixties, ten years after I first trekked around Ringim and Jahun, when education had spread far enough to encourage new tastes and soften resistance to change. What could I have not achieved!

We were never more than a few hundred in a land of millions, and in the fifties when we needed to insure that the roots of representative government in the district and village councils had been well pressed down, watered, and fertilized, and to tackle so many tasks in the native authorities, our dwindling numbers were perforce more and more pulled away from the people to the necessary support of the tall and rapidly growing tree of state. Constitutional advance at the center was so swift (albeit not swift enough for some) that the periphery had to suffer in the division of resources. When, six years after independence, representative government toppled, brought down by contempt of those in power for its roots as much as anything else, stability and order once again depended upon the district and village heads, their administrative capacity enlarged under British rule but the basis of their authority much as it had been before our arrival. The native authorities had, through lack of care for which no one can really be blamed, not kept up with the general pace of modernization.

But we had built an administrative structure, improving upon what we found, and keeping its cogs turning as each new political development increased the strains. We left behind us an organization which survived revolution and counterrevolution, civil commotion and military disarray, for longer and far better than we could ever have hoped in an infant state with recently graduated leaders. Some in the service, too, were creators, men of imagination whose ideas are still the basis of much that is good in the economic and social development of the country. Less obvious, but of importance to the generation of Nigerian civil servants which succeeded us, was our example. We did not always teach very well in a direct way, but we were watched day and night as we went about our business and pleasures. Our behavior set a pattern and established a standard which has survived. Even now the few who remain carry this particular burden. This is the real difference between a service and a group of mercenaries. The many experts of all nationalities who have flooded into Nigeria since independence can do a useful job but they have no involvement. They offer a skill not themselves, and they offer it as individuals, not as part of a team.

It might perhaps have been easier with so short a time available under a system of direct rule. But indirect rule was not so much a policy as a necessity, and we turned, over the years, necessity into a virtue. Certainly our frustrations as young men derived as much from the limitations of working indirect rule as from the inevitable irritation of young for old or difficult climate and poor conditions.

Joyce Cary's description in *Aissa Saved* of Bradgate, the DO Yanrin, and his encounter with the Emir Jibrin over bridging the river Akoko accurately and skilfully depicts similiar scenes in all our careers. When I read of Bradgate, in anger and despair charging into the muddy Akoko to show what is needed and making of himself an object of disgust and contempt to the watching NA officials, I think of an encounter of mine when I was ADO, City, in Zaria. The treasury had no long-carriage typewriter, needed for typing certain accounts. Funds were available for new typewriters. I pointed out the need. My advice was listened to politely and ignored. New machines were purchased from the agent most prepared to return a portion of the payment, rather than on their quality or suitability. None had a long carriage. I did not give up. I discovered that the chief of police had a long-carriage machine in his clerk's office, and no particular need for it. I suggested an exchange with one of the new treasury typewriters. All agreed, but nothing happened. Neither treasurer nor chief of police seemed able to carry out this simple and minor administrative adjustment, and it did not seem to me to be the kind of matter which we should encourage for decision by emir and council, rulers of three-quarters of a million people. A few weeks later there came a time when the treasury just had to get its annual accounts typed, and I was told that lack of a long-carriage typewriter would make it impossible. I begged and cajoled in vain. In desperation I made the necessary entries in the stores ledger, picked up the typewriters myself and moved them. I had thought that I might at least shame someone into helping me carry one of the machines. I received instead looks of withering contempt.

What I liked least about indirect rule was its power to corrupt. One could easily be turned into a Pontius Pilate. But if one resisted this temptation it was a good discipline. With a direct command impossible, I had to learn how to carry people with me over painful weeks of negotiation, letting them believe that the object of our discussions was their own idea and project. I found that the more positive I was, the easier I could achieve success. Even the most conservative and unco-operative chief or official had some goal toward which he could be persuaded to work with a little bit of enthusiasm. It only needed identifying. So I tried always to subordinate the negative and inspectoral side of my duties to the opportunities for creative action. When I visited a district, for example, I always left the necessary routine cash checks until the end of my stay. To have begun with them would have put an unfair strain on my relationship with the DH and perhaps inhibited progress in other affairs of more constructive purpose, because in a country without easy credit and of universal improvidence it was the custom to borrow from the office safe until the end of the month. Given time the DH could usually rally round sufficient to make good the deficiency until I was over the horizon. I avoided having to accuse an experienced administrator of embezzlement, but he nonetheless had a warning not to overdo it, and I gained the good will without which there could never be the development which would, by raising standards of living, eventually reduce the necessity for petty peculation.

The discipline of indirect rule, the constant searching for an area in which co-operation could be guaranteed and progress made, taught one tact and discretion. It was also a good training for those of us who were to stay on in the civil service after independence and serve a sovereign Nigerian government. Indeed more British did remain in Northern Nigeria for longer than in other former British colonies. Our apparently deeper involvement in the country and with its peoples than was usual elsewhere, including Southern Nigeria, has been often commented upon.[1] As well as the training in diplomacy it gave us, indirect rule made us a buffer between the people we served and higher authority rather than the direct agency of authority itself, and so, perhaps, we grew more possessive of those in our care. Certainly we all, quickly and deeply, identified ourselves with the cause of those we immediately served. In Kano it was the districts I toured

1. See for example, J. P. Mackintosh, *Nigerian Government and Politics* (London: Allen and Unwin, 1966).

which mattered most to me and on whose behalf I would fight with vigor. It was the same in Zaria, but there, in the pagan districts, I also identified myself with the cause of the former slave peoples. When it came to supporting Zaria NA against the regional government, however, I did so, even though I was a servant of that government. We hated to oppose an NA on behalf of the government, while we happily fought the NA on behalf of a district! The loyalties of the man in the provinces worked upward; it was for the man in the Secretariat to have a loyalty which worked downward, although he too would be expected to champion the Region against the Federation, and North against South.

This strong regional loyalty of the expatriate civil service may perhaps have helped to institutionalize the sad relations between Nigerians in North and South. The distrust has been most tragically manifested in the clash between Eastern Ibo and Northern Hausa, first in Kano in 1953 and then on a far wider and more terrifying scale since 1966. I had always hoped that Western education, common styles of urban living, the increasing acceptance among the young of new international tastes and standards, and the necessity after the British withdrawal of working out their own compromises and finding a new referee, would bring the many peoples of Nigeria ever closer together. In a sense I was right. It is much harder today to distinguish Northerner from Southerner than it was when I first arrived in Nigeria and dress alone was sufficient to differentiate them. But there was ample opportunity for bitterness to grow between communities which did not mix easily let alone integrate, in which one group held the political power and another seemed to win most of the economic prizes.

A Kano DH was once asked by a colleague of mine, soon after the riots of 1953, what would happen after independence. "We will kill all the Ibos and drive the rest of the Southerners into the sea," was the reply. Knowing how the Ibos had fought in Kano, I never took the comment seriously. How wrong I was the events of 1966 were to prove. Personally I always had Southerners as well as Northerners among my friends, although my work took me more among the latter than the former. I can also see much that is admirable and needed in the country in the Ibo characteristics of drive and thrift. Northerner and Southerner can so usefully complement one another rather than compete that it is doubly tragic that a *modus vivendi* has so far proved out of reach.

Our loyalty to the Region tended to make us side with the Northerner in the tribal clash. In colonial times he seemed to need so much protection from his go-ahead and technically advanced Southern fellow countryman. Living in the North we did not have to face the aggressive side of the nationalist feelings of the Southerner except occasionally in the bigger towns. A friend once wrote to me from Kano, of which he was very fond, saying that he felt he must get away to a smaller place "where there isn't a *sabon gari* to turn me into a Malanist." Expatriates in the South often told us how lucky we were to work in the part of the country where the people were so polite and race relations so good. Relations were as good as they were, perhaps, because by and large there were none, except between a handful of senior officials and the local aristocracy. Privately the Moslem Northerner regarded the generality of Europeans as barbarians, little better than the pagans whose nudity we allowed even our women to emulate at the swimming pool. He despised our way of life of which he wanted no part, convinced of the superiority of his own. We were left free, as a consequence, to live our life as we wanted, unmodified by local influence or prejudice. The two communities left each other in peace as far as their leisure hours were concerned. For years only the polo field provided a social meeting point, and then for the game alone, not for the exchanges in the club bar afterward.

In the South it was very different. The Southerner wanted to join in, to enjoy what we enjoyed. He cast envious eyes on our tennis courts and swimming pools. He even wanted to share our religion. A Southern clerk once told me, in answer to my inquiry why he had come a long way round to my house, that he could not bring himself to cycle past the club and see the whites playing tennis where he could not. The Middle Belter, as he too began to taste Western education and accept more of its values than did

at first his more Northern brother, tended to share the feelings of
the Southerner. As a result it was easier for those of us who
belonged to the time of transition, had a stake in the Nigerian
future, and wanted to know Nigerians as fellow human beings
rather than just as pleasant people one administered to get to
know him. Sympathy of mind, the essence of friendship, was
much more possible. It was also easier to quarrel with a Middle
Belter, something we did much less rarely with a Hausa or Fulani. Of course there were many individual exceptions to a gener-
alization of this kind, and the pattern is always changing as the
younger generation in the far North becomes increasingly Western in outlook. Indeed, in the sixties the most sophisticated elite
in a Western sense are often Fulani, and a good Fulani is quite
outstandingly good because he shines not just in his own right but
in that of a tradition.

So long as the colonial government continued, our rather eccentric but understandable pattern of loyalty seemed to work.
From governor down we belonged to the same breed; every man
among us had his first loves and sacred memories. Politics was to
put an impossible strain on the system except for the very few
who were able, because of former associations or a particular
experience, not only to serve the government of the day loyally
but also to espouse fully the cause of the party in power. After the
period of which I write, I was to find that my loyalty to certain
individuals, to a district, an NA, the Region, the Federation, and
the British government could easily come into conflict. I sometimes found myself answering Nigerian friends who inquired
whether I was thinking of leaving Nigeria that if I did so it would
be either because I was not by nature an imperialist, whether
British or Fulani, or because I had no intention of becoming a
white slave. But, to be fair, in my own case I was never asked to
do anything which offended my conscience, and if I worked hard
it was because of my own willingness to do so. I was always able
to tell my students, worried about future political pressures on
them as administrative officers, that if you have a reputation for
incorruptibility no one will ever try to corrupt you. I also was able
to reassure those of humble or minority ethnic origin that really

hard work could earn rewards as rich as those of patronage—and the more satisfying because honestly won.

But most of these problems the service as a whole did not have to face. As independence drew near the British government insisted on generous compensation schemes for those who might not wish to serve on. In practice it was almost impossible for the man in mid-career with children to educate not to take his lump sum compensation and go. "Lumpers," as we called it, finished the service. Nigerianization of the civil service was a necessary part of independence, but everyone was far too shortsighted about the expansion economic growth stimulated by independence was going to bring. Within a few years the British government was involved in recruiting and financing a new group of technical assistance personnel to take our place. Other governments were asked to do the same and the "new Europeans," as we called them, flooded in. Others were hired direct. Nigerians, at first, thought these new-type expatriates, would be easier to handle than the old service. But you cannot build a worthwhile public service with mercenaries and short-term foreign experts. Involvement is necessary and its advantages far outweigh its disadvantages. Only by involvement can you expect standards to be set, and the expatriate offering Western skills must do this both professionally and personally if he is to be of any value at all. How much better it would have been to have formed a new Commonwealth Service for those of us prepared to carry on, sustaining the involvement, providing the necessary security, resolving the conflict of loyalties, and fulfilling the needs of the country at probably far less cost.

It is all too easy to be wise after the event. At the time, for me, the job itself was challenging and satisfying enough. Independence was a goal I could accept and work for with a will. I only wish that the exciting new prospects it opened up could have been presented as a challenge just as satisfying. My career thereafter seems in many ways an anticlimax, but that is a story for future telling. For the present I am content to think back to the best of the bush days. As I travel about Nigeria I recall with affection and respect my former colleagues whose spirits must surely lurk still in the trees we all planted, little groups of lonely mangoes marking the site of former resthouses, handsome avenues of mahoganies lining the horse ride from house to city gate, and the leafy shade of the neem bringing cool shadows to the dusty desert towns.

Touring Reports

The following pages are a selection of the reports I wrote during my cadet days. I have included them to assist those interested in the detail of an administrative officer's work who do not have the opportunity to read such reports in the archives. A particularly rich and varied collection of material is available in the Bodleian Library at Oxford University. Many former colonial civil servants have deposited their diaries, correspondence, and other personal papers with the Institute of Commonwealth Studies for the benefit of the collection.

From studies of these papers the true image of the service will eventually emerge. Then, as the reports in these pages show, it will be seen that we were essentially developers. A myth has grown up, encouraged especially by those who have tried to turn public administration into an academic discipline and are engaged in teaching future African administrators, that colonial administration was concerned only with law and order. We were, of course, concerned with law and order and the early soldier-administrators no doubt gave it first priority. But read their reports. They were quickly and vitally concerned with the encouragement and development of trade and communications. The critics, perhaps because they travel by air themselves, forget that the railway between Lagos and Kano, begun in the first decade of British rule, was completed before the end of the second. No five-year plans indeed, but how many developed countries thought in terms of economic planning before the 1940's?

I and my contemporaries certainly conceived of our role as one of development, and not of pacification. The basis of the economic infrastructure, which latter-day economists scorn as so slight, had to be laid by somebody. The first road is the most difficult to build, the first school the hardest to fill. The back of the task had been broken long before the first economic expert arrived on the scene. Admittedly colonial governments were by nature overcautious and in West Africa determined to avoid unscrupulous Western exploitation. That was to come after independence. And it was after independence in Nigeria that the government of the day found itself more and more involved in the administration of security and less and less in the administration of development. My Nigerian successors, rather than my British predecessors, have been the administrators who have had to devote most of their energies to the maintenance of law and order.

Monthly Report: Northeastern Touring Area, Kano Division

Ringim District

1. Administration

(a) *Jangali:*[1] Compared with the same time last year *jangali* is down. The DH and VH explain this by saying there are few nomad cattle this year, and a large number of deaths due to disease among settled herds. I visited most of the village areas where *jangali* showed the greatest discrepancies with last year's figures, but found no hidden cattle. Correct receipts were produced on every occasion. I am inclined to support the theory that owing to the late rains cattle moved up to the remoter areas later than usual and are still on the move. The following table gives a comparative view of *jangali* figures this year and last.

	3 Sept. 1951	3 Sept. 1950
Home:	14,595	16,790
	(£2,554)	(£2,838)
Nomad:	782	2,721
	(£136)	(£476)
Total:	15,377	19,511
	(£2,690)	(£3,414)

(b) Complaints: There is a well-organized and quite open "cell" of NEPU[2] in Ringim town. Members of this whom I saw were all Hausa. The *yan Nefu* presented me with a list of complaints all of which seemed reasonable and fair. They were as follows:

(i) State of the market (see under section 5 below).

(ii) State of the wells (see under section 6 below).

(iii) Lack of drugs in the dispensary (see under section 4 below).

(iv) Cost of *Ijara*[3] court fees. This complaint appears justified from

1. Cattle tax.
2. Northern Elements Progressive Union, the opposition party.
3. The charge for the summoning of witnesses in a civil suit.

the list of fees in the District Note Book. Although the list is dated 1934, the fees seem to have risen out of all proportion to the rise in the cost of living. E.g., the fee for Ringim town in 1934 was 1*d*. Now it is 1/7*d*.

Complaints received from individuals—most of them NEPU according to the DH—were few and are being dealt with.

(c) Police: The stationmaster and traders in Ringim are all concerned at the number of thefts in the canteen[4] area. These reach their peak in the produce season. The four NA police stationed at Ringim appear to be ineffective other than in keeping order during the arrival and departure of passenger trains. As Ringim handles more produce than any other station between Kano and Nguru it does seem that during the produce season at least some more effective form of policing is required.

The canteen area at Majia has no police at all. It is the only station without police in the touring area. The stationmaster is anxious that at least two should be stationed here. There have been a number of thefts in the past few months.

(d) Prisons: The prison at Taura is in a very bad state of repair. It is not a good building and the cost of thorough repairs now would not be much less than the cost of a new prison. The *alkali*[5] holds court at Taura frequently. Immediate cleaning of the prison compound and the provision of latrines is to be undertaken.

(e) Postal agency: Negotiations for a postal agency at Taura have been proceeding for a year. The railway authorities are prepared to allow the stationmaster to act as postal agent, and to use the station safe, and it would seem that this is a satisfactory arrangement. It works at Ringim. The main use of a postal agency at Taura would be during the produce season and so, if it is to be of use this year, an early settlement is desirable.

(f) Resthouses: The northeast wall of Taura resthouse has fallen down.[6] A complete new wall will be necessary. The building is also in need of routine repair and whitewashing. The metal frame structure is still sound. As this resthouse is much used in the produce season by commercial agents it would seem desirable for immediate repairs to be effected.

2. Agriculture

(a) Crops: Groundnuts are now being pulled throughout the district. At Taura the Yemeni traders had started buying by the twenty-

4. Trading posts, buying produce and selling goods.
5. The judge of a Moslem court.
6. My diary records that this happened with me in it, the wall luckily falling outwards after the resthouse had been struck by lightning in a thunderstorm one night.

fourth. Except in the far east millet has been fully harvested and everywhere, though particularly south of the Hadejia River, guinea corn promises to be excellent.

(b) Artificial fertilizer campaign: The Captain of the Ringim fertilizer team has been touring with me this month. Marked enthusiasm has been shown by the *talakawa*[7] for the fertilizer. They are now able to compare results with the promises and in all cases appear more than satisfied. Independently of my visiting farms which had a free issue, I have heard talk in markets etc. which leads me to believe that providing there is the fertilizer to buy and the ready cash it will be bought, and not only by those who had it this year, but by others too.

At the same time several farmers have pointed out to me that they will not buy the pellet fertilizer stocked in some of the canteens. They received powder fertilizer this year and are in no way convinced that the pellet variety is as good. There is the additional point that they have received instruction in spreading the powder form but not in using the pellets.

(c) Demonstration farm, Taura: This farm is excellently run and has a splendid display of crops this year. The farm buildings are, however, singularly delapidated and will need attention as soon as the rains are over.

3. *Education*

(a) Ringim school: Repairs are needed immediately to the ceiling and walls of one of the brick classrooms. Otherwise the school appears to be running smoothly.

(b) Taura school: The only apt description of this school is "pathetic." One of the two buildings is so bad that I very much doubt if it will survive to the end of the rains. The other is not much better. Both are filthy. There are no latrines. The headmaster complains that his requests for school materials do not receive attention. There is no football, though I very much doubt if it would be used. Books required correction, and the preparation book began anew to coincide with my arrival. It would appear that an early visit to this school by an education officer is necessary.

(c) Sankara school: The buildings of this school have been erected and staff engaged. Both have remained idle for six months now, awaiting an official opening by the Emir. If an early visit by the Emir is not anticipated I would suggest that classes be recruited immediately and the school opened. The Emir would then be able officially to open a "going concern" at a later date. The staff are at present swelling the ranks of Ringim school.

7. Peasantry. Nobody liked to talk about peasants so we always used the Hausa word.

(d) Ringim reading room: This is a very good building but again in need of repair. The emphasis is, however, very much on the "room" and not on the "reading." There are a total of 111 books including J. E. Neale's *Elizabethan Parliaments!* Magazines and newspapers are non-existent. At present, in fact, the salary of the malam in charge seems a complete waste of money. At the same time there is a public for a reading room in Ringim.

4. *Medical*

(a) Ringim dispensary: A medical officer visited the dispensary during August but there appears to be a distinct shortage of some drugs. The complaint of NEPU is to this extent fair. On the other hand I was told that the medicines were ineffective—a complaint about which I can do little! The filter is broken and requires replacement. The incinerator is not in use except as a growing ground for *kashin yawo*.[8]

(b) Village sanitation: The growing of crops in compounds is the general rule in Ringim District. But in many places, and in particular Taura, it goes further and there are high crops, usually millet or *rama*,[9] in many of the streets completely blocking the way even for pedestrians.

5. *Markets*

(a) Ringim market: This market is large and important. It is not very satisfactory at present. It would be an admirable place to build a new market with the raised stall. Certainly the slaughter slab needs replacing this year. It is old and broken. (Incidentally it is the only concrete slab other than the one at Taura in the whole district.)

(b) Taura market: Most of this market is under water for twenty-four hours after rain. Simple drainage would improve the position. The slaughter slab is some three hundred yards away on the other side of the railway—and near the resthouse. It is a good slab but would be far better sited nearer the market. Alternatively, when it can be afforded, a new site for the market, on higher ground, and out of the town, would be a great improvement.

(c) Kore: There has been no market at Kore since the village was opened up some seven years ago. The nearest markets are at Fagen Gawo and Kiri. The VH and *talakawa* are very anxious to have a market. As Kore is so close to Majia railway station I would suggest a site between the two. Majia has no market but is only three miles from

8. Literally, to "kill walking." The name for the South American star weed, *Acanthospernum hispidum*, introduced into Nigeria in fiber sacks and spreading at an alarming rate.
9. A plant used to produce fiber.

Kiri. The station is another two miles farther away. That there is a need for this market I have no doubt. At present an unofficial market meets around the railway line every week. It would serve a considerable area.

6. Water supplies

(a) Ringim town: There are only six wells in Ringim including one at the station. They are old and in a bad condition. At present most people draw water from the floodwaters of the Hadejia River and its tributaries which come right into the town during late August and September. There is a definite need for the provision of one or two up-to-date wells.

(b) Majia: The village well requires repair to the cement surround. It is dangerous at night and, in fact, a horse recently fell down it. The station well is used by the growing *sabon gari*[10] and dries up owing to overdrawing in the dry season. As Majia is being developed by the Nigerian Railway as a depot for engine drivers (building of houses is proceeding at present) it would be desirable if a well could be sunk in the *sabon gari*.

Jahun District

7. Administration

(a) *Jangali:* Compared with the last year *jangali* is down. There are plenty of nomad cattle about but of the several hundred I have inspected nearly all have only recently moved into the district and had paid *jangali* in Wudil District during July. To date a total of 15,364 cattle have paid tax, out of which only 886 were from nomad herds.

(b) Resthouses: Jahun resthouse is in a very bad state and uninhabitable during the rains. To make it so a complete new thatch will be required. The boys' huts all need major repairs. It would seem that in the long run it would be cheaper to build a new and smaller resthouse of the semipermanent design rather than to carry out annual maintenance on the present large one. This is the only resthouse being maintained in the district.

8. Agriculture

Crops are not very impressive in Jahun. Groundnuts have not yet begun to be harvested. Evacuation to the railway is a long and painful procedure until later, and road transport hardly plays a part until January.

10. The new town, the generic name for the strangers' settlements on the outskirts of all Hausa towns.

9. *Education*

The DH is very keen for a school at Aujara which is a large town with over six hundred taxpayers in the town itself. It would serve the western part of the district. The VH seems as keen as can be expected —he has held his present office since 1896!

10. *Medical*

(a) There is no dispensary in Jahun District and the DH has requested one. It certainly is necessary as Jahun is very isolated during the rains.

(b) Village sanitation: High crops are common in most villages, usually millet or *rama*.

11. *Water supplies*

Aujara has no cement-lined wells and there is an obvious need for them in so large a town.

Jahun
30 Sep 51

Monthly Report: Northeastern Touring Area, Kano Division

General

1. Administration

What must be a heavy item of expenditure for all departments of the NA appears to arise from the excessive visits to Kano made each month by various departmental officials. A district senior scribe may visit Kano four times within a month. (In lorry fares alone this amounts to £1 4s. od. in the case of Ringim.) Agriculture, forestry, and veterinary assistants are frequently away in Kano. Schoolteachers and dispensary attendants offend least. Apart from the expense of so much travel, valuable working time is lost in the districts.

I am of the opinion that officials often perform duties which could well be undertaken by the messengers who arrive and depart almost daily. (I have myself received *dogarai* on two consecutive days when neither brought a message of great importance or urgency, and within a day of returning to Kano when merely personal mail came out.)[1]

While personal visits will obviously remain important in a country of poor communications and a low standard of literacy it seems that district scribes could make more use of correspondence than they do. This also applies to departmental assistants. The attitude is prevalent that unless a visit is made nothing gets done—in fact, a vicious circle has arisen.

2. Agriculture

(a) Groundnut buying is in full swing and the railway centers are a hive of activity by day and the scene of merrymaking by night. Ringim attracts more farmers than anywhere else even when another trading area is closer. A remarkable number of middlemen seem able to carry on a good business within a few yards of the canteens. General

---

1. Crocker makes much the same comment. I was once woken up at three in the morning by an elderly messenger who had ridden at speed through the night to deliver my grocery bill. The distribution of messages and mail was in the hands of a delightful but illiterate chief *dogari*, named Makaddes. He worked on the principle that to Europeans all paper was of supreme importance.

opinion among the traders is that the crop will be double if not treble that of last season. A shortage of coin, in particular shillings, seems likely to occur between the present time and the collection of *haraji*.[2]

(b) Soil erosion measures are well carried out in this touring area. Grass or other strip planting around the boundaries of farms is almost 100 per cent. It is noticeable that closer to Kano farms are often enclosed—mud walls and thicket or thorn fences being used.[3]

(c) Hides and skins: The all but universal practice of *sarakunan fawa*[4] is to sun dry their hides. I thought at first that it was chance that frames were most frequently lying from north to south but have come to the conclusion that such is considered the correct method. With the full heat of the sun drying is completed very rapidly and to the detriment of the hide. If frames lie from east to west the process is longer but more even and the finished product superior. Considering the importance of the hide and skin industry in Nigeria, district heads might well be informed of the best method of drying.

3. *Communications*

To a considerable extent the poor condition of dry-season roads appears to be attributable to the method of repair commonly in use, unfortunately often under the supervision of an overseer who should know better. Where deep ruts require filling and leveling the earth for this purpose is scraped away from the sides of the road on either side of the bad patch, which is usually at the bottom of a dip in the road. This method of repair, therefore, levels off the ruts but does not raise the level of the dip and increases its surface area by scraping away the banks of the road so that more water than ever will lie after rain. The process is assisted by vehicles following the line of the road bank, and after a few years a considerable pond is formed. If the simple measure of collecting such earth as is necessary for repair work away from the road banks were taken much of this could be avoided.[5]

Gabasawa District

4. *Administration*

(a) Guruma village: A new area for this village has been approved by the Emir and medical authorities less than a mile away from the

2. The general or income tax.
3. This displayed my ignorance. The enclosed farms were dry-season cassava farms. They were enclosed because goats, kept tied up during the rains and general farming season, were allowed to graze freely after the harvest.
4. The village tanners. I was capitalizing on knowledge read in an article.
5. Not only is my comment far from clear but it displays my ignorance. Nobody really bothered about maintaining dry-season roads. In Kano they were sandy tracks worn down below the level of the surrounding farms. All attention was devoted to upgrading these roads to all-season by giving them a laterite surface.

present village and on the Kano-Gumel road. The present village is a collection of less than ten compounds, the majority of the *talakawa* living on their farms. In the village, the men assured me that they had no wish whatsoever to move and wanted to build a new village on the old site. The VH on the other hand is fanatically keen to move. The present site looks as though it holds water in the wet season and the move seems in every way desirable. If a new village is begun it seems likely that many will follow the lead of the VH and move, though at present the majority are adamant in their dislike of the idea. They could give me no reasons.

(b) Zakirai resthouse: This resthouse is uninhabitable. The roof has fallen in and all the boys' huts require major repairs. Although it is an old resthouse the state of the compound and the buildings are so neglected it is to be doubted if much or any repair work has been conducted for some time. In 1948 the resthouse was reported in good condition.[6] The need for a resthouse in this district is apparent.

(c) Gabasawa resthouse: At Gabasawa the state of affairs is rather worse. Not only has the roof fallen in but the walls are partly down. Again the boys' huts are in a hopeless state of ruin. The resthouse is not, however, much frequented (even by the caretaker) and seems such a total loss at present as to raise the question whether it is worth maintaining. It was used as follows in recent years:

Year	1945	1946	1947	1948	1949	1950	1951
Nights used	1	4	2	0	1	1	0

Zakirai is eight miles distant by motor road (dry season) and six by horse track. A good *zaure*[7] is obtainable in Gabasawa.

5. *Education*

Zakirai school: The school appears to be running smoothly and the buildings are in good order. The school farm has been used this year, it appears, largely to demonstrate economics; its single crop of groundnuts was stacked in nine sacks in the classroom as a visible reminder during my visit. I suggested to the headmaster that the encouragement of a varied and balanced diet and the teaching of sound agricultural principles were the main function of the farm.

6. *Forestry*

(a) I could discover no recent prosecutions for forest offenses. The interest of the *alkalai* tends, naturally enough, to be confined to

6. This gives an indication of how rarely this district, close to Kano, was slept in by administrative officers and of the decline in the use of the District Note Books from which I gleaned my information.

7. Entrance hut to a compound.

matters concerned with the *shari'a*[8] and there is little encouragement given to a forest guard who brings forward statutory offenders. Unless the fines for these offenses fill a local treasury it seems unlikely exhortations will be much heeded.

(b) Dagar and Guruma village areas have requested communal forest areas.[9] At village meetings the *talakawa* were in favor. In both cases, however, the motive was in no way connected with a desire either to stabilize and assure fuel requirements or to hand down forest to posterity. What interested the villagers was the "limited grazing" allowed in a CFA. If grazing was prohibited they would have been firmly against the establishment of a CFA.

7. Markets

(a) Gabasawa: The cement slaughter slab is in an unhygienic state of disrepair. It is ten years old.

(b) Garun Danga: This is the largest market in the district and is situated in the bush some two miles from the village. As many as fifty cows a day are slaughtered during the harvest. There is no cement slab although the need for one is clearly indicated. Owing to its size and remoteness I strongly recommend that a *sarkin kasuwa*[10] be appointed. The *sarkin fawa* is busy with the large amount of flaying and drying and the VH lives too far away to be effective. It was in a disgusting state five days after market day when I visited it. The DH is not keen on the idea of a *sarkin kasuwa*.

(c) The sanitary inspector has been instructed to encourage the sale of meat from tables, a simple sanitary measure which, as yet, has not caught on in this district.

8. Water supplies

Apart from the Hadejia River in the south, which would require mammoth works and skill, and the Jekada River in the north, which I have yet to see, there are no rivers which might be dammed.[11] At the same time the lack of water other than well drawn is a serious deterrent to mixed farming.

There are, however, plenty of *fadama*[12] which dry up early in the dry season. It would be fairly easy to dig tanks in these. The actual volume of water might be increased, although even if it were not, the surface area would be much diminished and loss by evaporation

8. The body of Koranic law.

9. Communal forest areas were small stretches of wooded land intended to give a community fuel and building poles.

10. Market overseer.

11. We had all been instructed to look out for dam sites. A successful dam had just been completed at Kumbotso.

12. The marshes which are very characteristic of Northern Nigeria. Some hold water all the year through, others even flow as rivers in the rains.

delayed. Two or three might be constructed this coming dry season as an experiment.

Jahun District

9. *Administration*

(a) District office: The existing office is within the DH's compound. He is anxious to build a new one outside, incorporated into a council chamber. If no other source of funds is available I think this will be the priority as far as the district council is concerned.

(b) The DH is anxious to have two more messengers on the establishment. There are at present six. In view of what I said in section 1 of this report an increase is neither necessary nor desirable.

10. *Agriculture*

In marked contrast to Ringim there is little enthusiasm for artificial fertilizer. The demonstration plot has been a failure as far as visual propaganda is concerned although I have not been told the results of weighing. Crops seem generally poorer in Jahun than in Ringim, and the *taki*[13] team at Ringim has been extremely well led and carried on a much more vigorous program. It is strange that in adjoining districts the opinion of the *talakawa* should be so different.

11. *Communications*

It is unfortunate that in a district where so much is of a high standard inaccessability remains the drawback to progress. The men of Jahun are road conscious and wherever one tours the difficulties of crop evacuation are loudly voiced. It is to be expected that the cry for a road will be prominent on the agenda for the new district council.

The most satisfactory route for communication between Kano and Jahun is via Aujara, Chaichai, and Gaya. At present the dry-season road following this route is poorly maintained. As the *jigawa*[14] ridges run east-west a road to the south is impractical. To the north the Jahun-Harbo-Majia road is impassable except during the period from January to June. It opens too late after the wet season to carry much groundnut traffic. This year a large portion of the produce has been evacuated by way of Kale, Shafar, and Ringim. This route involves two river crossings, and donkey is the only possible form of transport. The northern exits to the railway are inevitably bad due to the extensive flooding of the Hadejia River.

13. Manure. Fertilizer was known as *takin Ture*, European manure.
14. Large sand ridges extending for miles and making road building very difficult.

A report on the possibility of a road from Taura to Gunka will be submitted shortly.

12. *Education*

(a) Jahun school: This school is impressively run and the buildings are in good repair. Class 4 is forced to sit at desks intended for Class 1 as requests for high desks and chairs have met with no reply. This is a position which needs to be remedied at once. (High desks were supplied to the new school at Sankara where there is only Class 1 as yet.)[15]

(b) The two classes of Jahun school are the only educational facilities in the district. The DH is most anxious for expansion and Aujara offers a large population center in the western half of the district. Jahun might well be extended to a four-class school.

13. *Trading layout*

Aujara has requested that trading plots be laid out near the town. It seems unlikely that they would be taken up, however, unless an all-season road is built via Gaya. Local opinion seems to be that the government will build a road for traders but not for villagers, and the idea of plots is to kill two birds with one stone.

14. *Markets*

(a) The fairly remote village of Mogama in the southwest of the district has requested a market. At present markets in Dutse District are used.

(b) Both Jahun and Aujara markets are large and neither has cement slaughter slabs. These might well be provided out of district council funds.

15. *General*

Despite its remoteness and backwardness, Jahun is an extremely well-run district. The district council should prove of immense benefit.

Ringim District

16. *Administration*

(a) Pilot census: Yakasawa village area was chosen for a trial census. A full report will be submitted in due course.

(b) Salary of *sarkin bariki:*[16] The *sarkin bariki* at Ringim com-

---

15. Primary schools were either two- or four-class, the former recruiting a new class alternate years. Hence the return of Class 4 at Ringim to the desks they used in Class 1.

16. Caretaker. *Bariki* comes from the English word barracks.

plained of a three month's delay in the payment of his salary. He was paid while I was at Ringim, although then it was short. The leakage had occured while the money was in the hands of the senior scribe.

(c) Taura resthouse: The wall of Taura resthouse has been repaired.

(d) Dabi resthouse: The office requires reroofing, the boys' huts, kitchen, and *bayan gida*[17] require replacement, and the *soro*[18] is so completely infested with the more vicious species of red ant as to be uninhabitable. There is also a termite hill in one of the rooms. This resthouse has been little used in the past five years and now requires far more than the usual annual repair. I suggest that it be abandoned. A good *zaure* is obtainable in Dabi village. The DH does not favor any suggestion of abandonment of resthouses. Including Dabi, three remain from an original ten.

(e) Ringim resthouse: There is a refrigerator in this resthouse. It does not seem to be in working order. Unless an officer is stationed at Ringim permanently I suggest the withdrawal of the refrigerator which might be better used elsewhere. At present it is merely deteriorating. Its use to a touring officer using a horse as his transport is almost nil, as not more than one or two nights consecutively are spent at the resthouse.

17. Agriculture

The Agricultural Department creamery at Dabi was clean and neat when I visited it, there was however very little milk in evidence. Less than two gallons formed the day's total purchases. The VH informs me that the Fulani get a higher price elsewhere and so will not come. I understand the Agricultural Department is to experiment with a volumetric measure. This should be less open to abuse than the present system of weighing. At the suggestion of Mr. Kingshotte the DH will, in the meantime, occasionally send a representative to see that the correct price of 2d. per pound is offered.

18. Communications

(a) A recce for a possible road linking the present Gumel road with the Hadejia road northeast of the Ringim area has been made during the month and a separate report will shortly be submitted.

(b) NA ferry at Shafar: The NA pontoon ferry across the Hadejia River at Shafar carries a large number of passengers. On October 6 I estimated that a hundred donkeys, their loads and attendants crossed during the day, not to mention the passage of pedestrians. Ferry dues

17. Toilet, literally "behind the compound."
18. The name for a building roofed as well as walled with mud.

are 1*d.* per person, 3*d.* per animal, and 3*d.* or 4*d.* per load. Charges for crossing by gourd are lower. Price fluctuations are apparent. The dues are collected by the *sarkin ruwa*,[19] who has held office for fifteen years. He is not paid a salary by the NA but retains the full amount of the dues. While the river is still flowing and once the produce season has begun he must take between £3 and £5 a day.

19. *Education*

(a) Sankara school began work on September 23 with thirty-six pupils. It appears to be running smoothly although the headmaster complains of shortages of such materials as chalk. He also wants a cupboard. A visit by him to Kano does not seem to have had much effect.

(b) Taura school is still desperately in need of repair and as yet, I am informed, no sanction has been made.

(c) The headmaster of Ringim school is anxious for a bathroom on the premises. Three swings have been built at this school.[20]

20. *Markets*

Ringim market slaughter slab remains in the same insanitary condition that has called forth reports for over a year now. The DH informs me that he still awaits a sanction. With market held every other day and an average of twelve cattle slaughtered it seems essential that this defect be seen to with all possible speed.

21. *Medical*

The filter at Ringim dispensary still requires replacement. It has been in its present condition for some months. A medical officer noted the position in August.

22. *Railway*

The stationmaster at Dabi called my attention to urgent repairs needed at the station. The well requires dredging if it is to last the dry season out. He has communicated with the appropriate railway authorities and awaits a reply.

23. *Water supplies*

The position at Majia is likely to be serious this year. The well in *sabon gari*, locally dug, has just collapsed. This leaves the village well, already fully drawn and a return distance of three and a half miles

19. The chief waterman.
20. An evening activity for me while in Ringim.

from the *sabon gari*, and the station well, which is not good and much used as Majia is now a depot for engine drivers. Local concern is considerable and the DH has been to see what the situation is.

Taura
1 Nov 51

Monthly Report: Northeastern Touring Area, Kano Division

General

Administration

On the first of the month the NA police stationed at Dabi, Ringim, Taura, and Zakirai stations were recalled to Kano and not replaced. As the stationmasters had for some time complained of the police attached to their stations they were not unduly surprised. I had warned them all of the current policy of withdrawing NA police from the railway and I had suggested that they request railway police. It is however regrettable that neither the district heads nor the stationmasters were given the slightest official notice of the withdrawal.

2. At Ringim, however, the NCO and three constables posted to the station were replaced after a week, but told that their work in future was concerned with the town and not with the railway. The DH is worried as he cannot imagine what their new duties are supposed to be and the police concerned are unable to enlighten him. The one really useful function which they hitherto performed, keeping order during the arrival and departure of passenger trains, they no longer undertake.

3. Dabi station goods shed was burgled the night of the withdrawal. From past records it appears that the NA police have not been effective in guarding the station areas, and I have several times been told by stationmasters that they would not undertake night duty. The solution is obviously to post railway police under the authority of the stationmasters. It would seem that one section stationed at Ringim under an NCO could patrol the line either side, from Jogana to Majia. The posting of a single policeman without proper supervision is not recommended.

4. Unless specific duties are to be given to the NA police at Ringim I recommend their withdrawal as at present they are unable to occupy their time. (The new cotton market may need police supervision.)

Communications

5. Road repair gangs have been much in evidence in the area. However it seems that four out of every five gangs are content to trim

the verges and leave it at that. It is significant that the men tend to set out to work armed not with a hoe but a cutlass. Bad ruts are left while *kashin yawo* is cut, after it has seeded, and the grass trimmed down, which is really an unnecessary labor. At the same time it is generally voiced by district heads that road repair sanctions do not suffice. It appears that a large amount of paid labor is wasted due to the lack of trained and experienced supervision. The difficulties are, of course, great. One possibility would be the amalgamation of the small village gangs working under the supervision of a village scribe into larger gangs with a definite timetable of work under the supervision of a trained peg-boy. If this system were organized central authorities would know where and when district gangs were working and occasional supervision from Kano could be exercised.

Ringim District

Administration

6. Taura prison is extremely badly managed. As was reported in September considerable repair work is required. The prison then was also in an unsanitary condition. A visit some eight weeks later showed not the slightest improvement. The *salga*[1] remained uncovered and so forth. The warder regarded the situation as though it were a joke. I do not consider that he is a suitable person to work on his own in a remote prison without supervision. He should be employed under senior authority or in a district headquarters where the DH would be able to exercise supervision.

Agriculture

7. Ringim cotton market was opened on the fourteenth of November with only one registered buyer. The market is situated to the immediate south of the town market.

Education

8. Taura school: As reported in September this school is in a sorry state. It desperately needs repair and one classroom is at present in danger of collapsing. There were, however, many things well within the competence of the headmaster which required seeing to. There were no latrines, the classrooms were filthy and so on. A surprise visit some eight weeks later found the school in precisely the same state. There are still no latrines, there are piles of filth on the floor, and the compound is neglected. The preparation book was nearly three weeks behind, the figures in the register did not tally with the pupils in the

---

1. A deep pit latrine.

class, and I found books requiring correction from as far back as May. There were no recent corrections at all.

9. A visiting teacher last inspected this school in April. I strongly recommend further inspection by the Education Department. It does not seem that the headmaster is capable of holding his position. When I arrived he was busy repairing bicycles outside the classrooms, and the pupils appeared to be left to their own devices. He had taken no heed of my warning and suggestions made in September. Either he should be employed as an assistant in another school or sent on a refresher course.

Water supplies

10. The VH of Kiri complains of lack of wells. The area is extensively flooded during the rains as it borders the Hadejia River. This has apparently prevented much in the way of local well-sinking.

Jahun District

Administration

11. Village councils have all held their meetings and the opening of the district council in December is awaited.

Agriculture

12. The northeast corner of Jahun is extensively flooded during the wet season. There are large lakes, most of which retain water throughout the year. As a result very little land is available for millet and no groundnuts are grown. A certain amount of rice and cassava are grown. To prevent flooding most villages have built a dike and wall around the village itself and within this dry area date palms usually flourish. In the main, however, the inhabitants regard themselves as fishermen rather than farmers. Fairly considerable quantities of fish are railed daily from Majia to Kano and Kaduna.

13. This area might be opened up for agriculture by dikes and ditches. If the individual efforts of villages were co-ordinated much more land could be made available. Whether, however, it would be farmed in preference to the river and lake fishing is doubtful, although in bad years there is usually a food shortage. A proper survey would be necessary but the existence of the lakes and clear water channels should make it a possible task.

14. Little can be done to improve the fishing although if quantities were guaranteed a more efficient system of marketing might be considered. A marketing co-operative centered on Majia with contacts in Kano and Kaduna is a possibility. With organization it should be

possible to rail fresh fish at least as far as Kano. At present only dried fish is dispatched.

Education

15.   The headmaster of Jahun school has still received no reply to his request for high desks. Otherwise this school is running smoothly.
16.   Work has commenced on the site for a reading room.

Kano
30 Nov 51

A Leadership Course for Jahun
District Councilors

Introduction

It is an established principle of representative local government that the representative or council member has a two-way function to perform with respect to his constituents. The dual character of his responsibilities consists on the one hand of carrying forward the pleas, suggestions, ideas, the mandate of the community he represents, and on the other of bringing down orders, information, and propaganda. In advanced societies the limelight is upon the upward thrust of the machinery, and in practice the organs of public opinion, the press and the radio, perform the task of the downward thrust. In a country where broadcasting is unknown and where there is little enough to read for those who can, the second function of a community representative is of immense importance.

2. The report which follows is an attempt to suggest one way in which this responsibility of the leaders of representative local government, in a district where it has but recently been inaugurated, might be fostered.

Nature of the course

3. The course is designed for district council members in order to give them knowledge which will make their opinions as leaders respected, to encourage better standards of living, and to promote their personal development so that they do not merely represent the opinions of a community but are an active force for good in the formulation of those opinions. The primary function of the course is not to provide education in local government so much as education for the leaders in local government. In Northern Rhodesia an ambitious scheme of training for chiefs and councilors has been undertaken for some time at the Jeanes School, Lusaka. "They have received instruction in village improvements, the importance of clean water supplies, lessons in civics and their place in the administration of the territory, and an insight into how Native Treasuries are run."* There seems reason to suppose that a less spectacular scheme of training designed for the members of one district council alone would not only meet

with success but would bring the additional benefit of enhancing the prestige of the council and its members.

Objects

4. (a) To emphasize the dual nature of the district council and its members.

(b) To encourage a sense of responsibility by representatives toward their constituents.

(c) To enhance the prestige and add to the dignity of a newly formed council and to foster a spirit of unity and solidarity among its members.

(d) To demonstrate ways of good and better living, particularly in the spheres of agriculture and hygiene.

(e) To promote development and welfare in a backward area.

Program

5. (a) General: The program will need to be designed within the limitations of personnel and equipment which will be discussed later. The stress will be upon practical instruction with the constant use of visual aids. Besides the main themes chosen for the course—agriculture and hygiene—there should be room for other items, including those of a social nature, all of which will help to put across the less tangible values which it is hoped a course of this nature will bring out.

(b) Visits: Not much can be undertaken in the way of visits in an outlying district such as Jahun, but the council members could take the opportunity of visiting the elementary school which might well prepare an exhibition of work suitable to the occasion. Attendance at an adult literacy class could be included in the program.

(c) Agricultural theme: The subjects of soil conservation and mixed farming would rightly stress the main needs of the district. The following is a list of the sessions which could easily be held and organized with material available locally. They will be seen to be not ambitious.

(i) Demonstration of contour plowing. Right and wrong methods demonstrated by means of playlet.
(ii) Method of stopping gully erosion shown on site.
(iii) Demonstration of effects of sheet erosion and the use of hedging.
(iv) Demonstration of plowing by iron plow and cattle.
(v) Talk and film on care and feeding of cattle.
(vi) Show of simple "foreign" farm implements; playlet to show benefits of donkey cart.
(vii) Demonstration of how to sow with artificial fertilizer.
(viii) Talk and/or film on forest matters. Sand model to demonstrate a CFA.

(d) Hygiene theme: This is bound to be secondary to the agricultural and would occupy fewer sessions. Much depends on what films or filmstrips are available. The Colonial Film Unit has produced several films, e.g., on smallpox, which would be applicable. Talks on the common local ailments, such as guinea worm, and their prevention can be given. If possible a model of a well-laid-out village would be shown, or better a visit to one made. A demonstration of right and wrong compounds and ways of meat selling could be made in the town.

(e) Minor themes:

(i) Correct method of hide and skin drying demonstration.

(ii) Demonstration of the simple spinning wheel in use in Kano NA Prison.

(f) Social: The course must obviously be enjoyed by council members, and items of a purely social value would provide welcome breaks from working sessions. Although it is doubtful if a football eleven could be found among the councilors (few, indeed, would be the local government bodies that could do this), they might enjoy watching a match between Jahun town and Jahun rural. Cinema shows could include entertainment as well as educational films and a gramophone concert be given. A special market day should be held.

(g) Timetable of sessions: Generally speaking the early morning and late afternoon seem to be the best times for either demonstrations or talks. Cinema shows would of course be after dark. A suggested program is attached.

Organization

6. It is essential that the course be capable of organization on a district level. If its program is too ambitious for a district to carry the weight of organization then the course loses its character and would be better enlarged to an emirate level. It should be emphasized that the course is designed for district councilors and district councilors alone. It is also important that the fewer strangers the better, be they visiting distinguished persons or instructors. The more intimate and homely the course the greater its success is likely to be.

7. The touring officer and the district head would between them supervise and be responsible for the arrangements. Individual sessions would be under the charge of local NA departmental assistants. Thus agriculture and forestry assistants would provide their particular demonstrations and the sanitary inspectors the hygiene demonstration. Schoolboys might be enlisted to help with the playlets. The course would provide local officials with a welcome change from routine duties. It may well teach them something and should certainly inspire them to greater efforts in the future. Above all it would make them

feel important and they would have a visible proof that their work is recognized and appreciated. The loan of one or two assistants might be needed, although in every way it is better if instruction is given by familiar faces. The cinema operators would, of course, be outside the district team.

Equipment

8. (a) In nearly every case the necessary equipment could be found locally, e.g., a mixed farmer would loan his plow and cattle.

(b) The course would be an excellent occasion to use a cinema apparatus, and the report has been written assuming that one would be available. It would need to be powered from a vehicle, presumably the one in which it was carried.

(c) The loan of a donkey cart from the Agriculture Department and such other implements as that department recommended or was prepared to loan would complete the list of equipment.

Finance

9. This naturally enough is regarded as the stumbling block to many a fine paper scheme. There is no reason why it need cause worries here. A good case can be made that a course as outlined need entail no financial commitments whatsoever. The basis of such a case is the assumption that the work involved may be considered as a normal part of the duties of the officials concerned. The same, to an extent, may be said of equipment. If the Agriculture Department regards the loan of a donkey cart as part of its normal extension work there would remain the cost of transport. The cinema apparatus is, perhaps, in a different category. If Kano NA possesses suitable equipment and operators then their use on such a course would seem a legitimate part of their job and not call for reimbursement. On the other hand it may be necessary to hire, and in that case payment would be involved. It can, however, be seen that whatever funds would be required would be sufficiently small to be a just expenditure of district council funds. If they were provided from another source the council would gain materially but might, perhaps, lose in its sense of financial responsibility.

Preparation

10. Once the program was firm and the personnel organized, some six days immediately prior to the course would suffice. This field preparation would enable the touring officer to hold a full-dress rehearsal of the various demonstrations.

Location of course

11. The town of Jahun itself is the obvious place for the course to be held, and the hill slope to the north of the town, on which stands the

resthouse, would be an excellent site for demonstrations. The interior of the town would provide the scene for compound demonstrations.

Date and duration

12. With the stress on agriculture, the nearer to the planting season the better it would be. In every respect at time prior to and fairly close to the 1952 planting season would seem ideal.

13. If the course assembled one afternoon it would last the next three full days and disperse on the day after that. Three days would be sufficient and not so long as to allow the course to become monotonous or stale.

Conclusion

14. If the course should prove a success it might be tried elsewhere. It can, therefore, be regarded as a pilot scheme.

15. The emphasis throughout should be on visual instruction. It would be true to say that nothing suggested in the program is likely to be new to council members. Many may already be mixed farmers and so forth. But if they have heard the word before, this time they would see it demonstrated before them. At worst the same old pill would have been coated with sugar. The less tangible results that might accrue would, however, be new. They would have sprung from the basis of the whole scheme which is in itself new—the formation of representative local government.

16. If nothing else the course will serve to bring district councilors together for several days. Their knowledge of one another and of the district would increase and an opportunity would be given to the development of a district rather than a village spirit. If some eyes and ears are opened so much the better. Future courses could lay the emphasis more on civic responsibilities and the practice of local government. Courses of this nature are being held in Kenya at present.† If local government is to be a living reality and a dynamic force in the structure of a democratic country, training of its leaders is a first requirement.

Jahun
4 Nov 51

* C. M. N. White, "The Place of Training in the Development of African Local Government in Northern Rhodesia," *Journal of African Administration*, Vol. II (July, 1950).
† R. J. C. Howes, "A Kenya Experiment in Training for Local Government," *Journal of African Administration*, Vol. III (April, 1951).

Population Movement in Kano Province

The object of the investigation, with a view to a possible resettlement scheme, was to establish whether there is any migratory movement from the densely populated environs of Kano to the thinly populated districts in the south of the province.

2. The investigation was conducted in Ungogo, Kumbotso, Kiru, and Karaye districts. At Ungogo and Kumbotso an attempt was made to discover what emigration had taken place over the last twenty years and information concerning the emigrants, future emigrants, land shortage, surplus population, and the relationship between these districts and the city with respect to landholding. At Kiru and Karaye the reverse investigation was made.

3. One particularly unsatisfactory point about the investigation should be appreciated at the outset. Information obtained in Ungogo and Kumbotso of emigrants who had supposedly settled in Kiru or Karaye was not once confirmed. The accuracy of all information received is therefore open to doubt in detail. But the information received in all four places tallied sufficiently to allow general conclusions to be reached about the pattern of migration in recent years.

4. The report deals with the districts in turn and summarizes conclusions. Tables are included in the text, and graphs and charts as appendixes.

Ungogo

5. Total emigration over the last twenty years is estimated as 140. Table I below gives details. Women and boys under twelve are not included in these or subsequent figures.

6. The table above shows that migration has been mainly confined to the province. The interesting comparision is between those who left to farm elsewhere and those who made the short move into the city. Much of the emigration has been due to the building of Kano Airport on Ungogo land. Of a total fifty-one displaced only one decided to farm elsewhere. He is reported in Rano. Thirty-one went to the city and the rest to Hadejia for Koranic learning.

7. Table II shows the distribution within the province of the thirty-five who left to farm.

Table I

Destination	Reason for emigration	Number	
Out of province	Farming	7	
	Trading	12	
	Laboring	0	
	Religious	0	19
Within province	Farming	35	
exclusive of	Trading	2	
city and Ungogo	Laboring	0	
	Religious	23	60
To Kano city	Various	58	
Within Ungogo	Farming	3	

Table II

District	Number
Kiru	7
Karaye	9
Gwarzo	5
Tudun Wada	5
Rano	1
Birnin Kudu	8

8. Ungogo's population in 1950 was 45,161. Every available piece of land is cultivated. Nine hundred and forty-nine farms are reportedly farmed by city dwellers. The surplus population does not emigrate in large numbers but as can be seen in Appendix A emigration has increased over the years. The estimated 10,000 increase in population over ten years has partly been employed in laboring at the airport and in the city. The district surrounds the city on three sides, and at no point is the outer boundary more than a few miles from numerous laboring opportunities. Craftsmen and traders also travel into the city daily to sell their wares. The district is exceptionally quiet by day. Farms are small, but produce fetches high prices from the city.

Kumbotso

9. The position in Kumbotso is similiar to that in Ungogo but the attachment with the city is less marked. Kumbotso does not border the canteen area, the main employment location for laborers. Emigration over the last twenty years is estimated as 188. Tables III and IV give details.

Table III

Destination	Reason for emigration	Number	
Out of province	Farming	17	
	Trading	12	
	Laboring	12	
	Religious	8	49
Within province	Farming	70	
exclusive of	Trading	4	
city and Kumbotso	Laboring	13	
	Religious	17	104
To Kano city	Various	31	
Within Kumbotso	Farming	4	

Table IV

District	Number
Kiru	11
Karaye	8
Gwarzo	2
Tudun Wada	18
Rano	6
Kura	4
Danbatta	4
Ringim	1
Gabasawa	1
Dawaki	1
Sumaila	3

10. The city has attracted fewer migrants and just under half the total left to farm. Most of those leaving for religious motives went to Koranic schools in Hadejia. Five had set out on the pilgrimage overland. The movement of emigrating farmers has been almost entirely southward and with a preference for the southwestern districts. Emigration out of the province follows a similar pattern, the southern districts of Katsina and Zaria accounting for the majority.

11. Kumbotso's population was 46,127 in 1950, an increase of 12,000 over the last ten years. Land is highly cultivated and farms are small. Seven hundred and seventy-five farms are reportedly farmed by city dwellers. Not more than 250 are employed in the city, at Challawa power station, or on the Agriculture Department farm. Traders and craftsmen travel to the city daily but less so than from Ungogo.

12. The only "organized" migration took place from Kumbotso in

1949/50. Fourteen young men from Kureken Sani sought permission of DH and Emir to go and look for farmland elsewhere due to the poor harvest and food shortage of that season.

Kiru

13. One hundred and forty-one immigrants have been reported over the last twenty years. Of these about a third have settled in villages where they had relatives. As can be seen from Table V only one came from the city and none from Ungogo and Kumbotso, although according to sources in these districts, eighteen had emigrated to Kiru. There is apparently considerable movement between the southern districts themselves.

Table V

Origin	Number
City	1
Minjibir	3
Danbatta	1
Gezawa	1
Bici	19
Dawakin Tofa	6
Kura	23
Karaye	45
Gwarzo	1
Rano	2
Katsina Province	10
Within Kiru	23
Unknown	6

14. There is some possibility that the twenty-three immigrants from within the district had previously entered from outside and were making a second move, hence they have been included. All immigration has been for farming. No account has been taken of the handful of non-farming immigrants to Yako and Dan Gora stations. These are traders or transient railway personnel.

15. Considerable numbers of migrants are reported to pass through Kiru on their way farther south. The DH believes most find land in Zaria. This is a possible explanation for the missing men from Ungogo and Kumbotso.

Karaye

16. Fifty-three immigrants have been reported over the past twenty years, most of them accounted for by migration within the immediate vicinity of Karaye itself.

Table VI

Origin	Number
Dawakin Tofa	4
Wudil	2
Kura	2
Gwarzo	10
Kiru	7
Zaria Province	5
Katsina Province	8
Within Karaye	15

17. Again there is evidence that the internal movement within Karaye was a second movement of migrants who had come in from elsewhere, and the figure has been included on this count.

Conclusions

18. There is migration from the immediate surroundings of the city where land is scarce, but it is far from being a significant percentage of total population. Movement is more likely into the city and away from farming in Ungogo and Kumbotso. The next line of districts, however, where land is also becoming scarce, such as Minjibir, Dawakin Tofa, and Gezawa may be sources of future emigrant farmers.

19. The general movement of migrating farmers is south and west. Kiru and Karaye have not received many immigrants. In Rano, without specific investigation, the opinion is that there have been few. In Tudun Wada, the most southerly and least densely populated district, the DH reports large numbers of immigrants.

20. Appendixes B and D give an impression of age groups of migrants. The majority are between twenty and forty and have farmed for some years before making the move. Under twenties in Ungogo, as can be seen in Appendix B, opted for the city.

21. Appendixes A and C show that migration is recent with a peak year in 1949/50. A food shortage seems the necessary incentive. Farmers asked in Ungogo or Kumbotso whether they had any thoughts of moving all seemed content, admittedly in the midst of an ample harvest. They are also reluctant to move away from the attractions of the city.

22. Pressure on land will no doubt continue to increase and a time will come when farms cannot stand further division. The amount of land litigation provides a useful thermometer.

23. Weighing the above factors, a limited settlement scheme in the southwest might be worthwhile. Knowledge that land was available and that others were moving might persuade marginal migrants that a

move would solve their problems. Others who would move into Zaria Province might be induced to stay within the province.

24. A scheme should be located where extension will be possible in the future as land pressure increases. A bad season, such as 1949/50, could set considerable potential into actual migration.

25. The lack of evidence of large-scale movement to new farmland means that costs of any scheme may prove to be a heavy burden for the benefit of a very small minority. But for the kind of man who left Kumbotso in search of better land in 1949/50 a scheme is needed and would be worthwhile. Merely putting land at their disposal would fail to capitalize upon their initiative in seeking new land. They would need credit for clearing, housing, and implements, and must be supervised on the spot if success is to be achieved.

26. The investigation was not detailed enough to discover whether many of the migrants had moved because they were the worst farmers and thus least able to stand up to the pressures of land hunger. It is likely some fall into this group, especially among the older men. Some form of selection would be necessary to get the best men, who would be the most likely to gain from exposure to improved techniques that a settlement scheme provides.

Kano
18 Dec 51

A Resettlement Scheme in Kiru District

Introduction

The following report is written to provide a basis for discussion of the resettlement scheme it is hoped to establish in Kiru District. The particular problems, both agricultural and administrative, of the area chosen in 1951 as suitable for settlement, as well as more general problems of resettlement are considered.

2. A geographical and administrative description of the area forms the first part of the report. The second suggests a possible scheme, and the final deals with the immediate steps that must be taken if resettlement is to begin this year.

The resettlement area

3. In July, 1951, Mr. Kingshotte of the Department of Agriculture toured Kiru District in order to find an area of virgin bush suitable for agricultural development. The area he chose lies east of the railway at Dan Gora and is bordered by the villages of Gwarmai, Sata, Kuki, and Gajale.

4. Mr. Kingshotte's report should be referred to for an assessment of the soil. A more detailed survey in January, 1952, has revealed that the area contains more farms than was previously supposed. It also seems probable that the depth of soil in large areas of granite under-rock would be insufficient to maintain crops. A number of small streams and one large one flowing southwest to northeast through the area are narrow and have rocky beds. An occasional natural dam holds water throughout the dry season. The water supply attracts cattle Fulani in large numbers and enables tributers from the mines southwest of Gajale to engage in a limited amount of mining close to Gajale itself. The area is a potential minesfield. There is a rich variety of game and tsetse flies are present. There is no evidence, however, of trypanosomiasis in either man or cattle. A list of trees is contained in Appendix B.

5. There is evidence of recent immigration and farmers are extending southward from Gwarmai into the area. The path from Gwarmai to Gajale seems to be an important trade and migratory route. Primarily a guinea corn area, groundnuts and some millet are grown. Cotton

is a popular crop after first clearing of new farms. Its possibilities as a second cash crop to groundnuts seem worth investigation.

6. Administratively the area falls into three village areas, Gwarmai, Gajale, and Kuki. The greater part of it lies within Gwarmai. The village heads and people showed every sign of pleasure at the prospect of a resettlement scheme. They feel it will bring prosperity and some are anxious to become mixed farmers.

7. Communications are bad. The road from Dan Gora to Gajale could be improved, but from there completely new tracks would be needed.

The scheme

8. The object of the resettlement scheme is to provide land for emigrants from the overcrowded environs of Kano city, controlling settlement so that the best agricultural methods are followed and thereby providing a higher than average standard of living.

9. A settlement scheme cannot be insulated from its immediate surroundings. Moreover it is desirable that it should not be regarded as something apart and unattainable except for the privileged. The physical boundaries of a scheme should not become the limit of its influence. The ultimate success of a scheme should be the point when farmers outside adopt the principles of good farming and living within the boundaries and thereby break them down.

10. For this reason it seems desirable that the larger area within which the scheme would be located be declared a development area and receive sufficient attention to enable it to keep up. A sharp contrast should be avoided.

11. Until the survey at present in progress is completed it would be unwise to select the actual acreage for the initial scheme. It is, however, almost certain that farms will lie within the area and a solution must be found to the problem they present. The best plan would be to take these farmers into the scheme. There would be opposition by some to the idea of moving perhaps only a few yards. For these compensation might be provided and land selected within their own village area outside the scope of the scheme.

12. It is suggested that the scheme be designed in the first place for a hundred families.

13. Kano men prefer village living and it is proposed that two villages be included in the layout of the scheme.

14. If higher productivity is to be obtained it is essential that mixed farming be introduced. Twenty acres per farm with communal grazing facilities is suggested. There is much to be said for a larger acreage and individual grazing, but the practice is to graze communally and fencing would be simpler. At Daudawa no provision for grazing was

made and it has remained a problem. Although it is proposed that farmers live in villages and not on their farms (as at Daudawa) provision for stalling of cattle on the farms is necessary. A suggested plan of farm layout and a design for a cattle stall are attached as Appendixes C and D.

15. A demonstration farm, or rather holding identical to that given to the settlers, should be established centrally under the supervision of either an agricultural assistant or a selected farmer. After a time it might be exchanged for another holding so as to give as many settlers as possible a chance to farm alongside the demonstration. No experiments should be conducted and it must be farmed with the same labor and tools as the average farm.

16. Two communal forest areas, one for each village, should be included.

17. Village layout should be regulated to improve standards and a plot 100 by 100 is suggested. They could be smaller and at Shendam plots are only 40 by 50. Live fencing should be provided at the start. Provision for a school, clinic, and administrative building should be included in the village layouts.

18. For both farm and compound, settlers should be issued with a right of occupancy containing the necessary clauses to prevent abuse and to allow supervision.

19. A cement-lined well in each village should be provided before the first settlers arrive. The rivers are easily controllable due to rocky beds and narrowness. Check dams would control runoff after rain and could supply cattle watering points.

20. Credit for purchase of plow, cattle, and the first year's seed will be needed. If the cattle are to be cared for a permanent stall is also needed. Repayment of credit should be made on a date to be fixed annually and should be identical for all after the results of the harvest can be seen and current prices are known. A settler who suffered some particular hardship would be allowed to appeal. At Daudawa many settlers are years in arrears. A firm arrangement and the right of eviction as a sanction are necessary.

21. Some initial help in the way of free fertilizer, citrus plants, etc. might be given in the first few seasons.

22. Clearing will cost money. Twenty acres is more than a family could clear for its own use in one or two years. Rooting might take many years before completion. Mechanical plowing is limited until rooting is complete. It seems that mechanical clearing is necessary.

23. Work on clearing and providing roads and bridges could provide a cash income for settlers during the dry season.

24. To get the best type of farmer for the scheme some form of

selection committee under the chairmanship of the agricultural officer will be necessary.

25. The administration of the settlement area presents a number of problems. In the first place somebody must be found to administer credit facilities and provide on-the-spot assurance that protective measures are obeyed. At first the assistant running the demonstration holding might suffice. Later he would need the assistance of a clerk. For this reason a small office is needed in the villages which villagers will recognize as their administrative center.

26. The scheme will eventually cut across several village areas. It is obviously undesirable that the settlers with common problems and perhaps internal disputes should be subject to more than one village head. A revision of the existing village boundaries is one solution, but far more satisfactory would be to treat the advanced living of a settlement area as deserving of some measure of self-government.

27. Settlers will come from several districts and find themselves among strangers. An excellent opportunity would be offered for the establishment of representative local government. A settlement head and committee could be elected, possibly every two years, by the settlers. The settlement head should be given village head status. The district head and *alkali*'s court would exercise normal jurisdiction.

28. If this experiment in self-government were made, the prospects of a community spirit developing are good. After a number of years it might prove possible to establish a co-operative society to provide credit (perhaps even taking this right out of government hands), cheap transport for crops, and a retail store.

29. In terms of general development of the area, road improvements, fertilizer distribution, and the creation of CFA's would, at first, provide the development proposed in paragraph 10.

Action required

30. When the survey is completed it will be possible to delineate the settlement area. It should then be beaconed and declared an agricultural reserve, investing the right of occupancy in the appropriate authority. While Kano NA is the obvious authority for settlement schemes it may be desirable to initiate these schemes and thereafter to decide policy by means of a committee which includes the divisional and agricultural officers. In this way the selection of farmers would be removed from the authority of any one individual.

31. It is suggested that the scheme begin this year with a small number of settlers, not more than twelve in number. There is little time left before the planting season, and the first year will be hard for any settler with new land to cultivate and a home to build. The

demonstration holding will need a year to settle down before it can do its work effectively.

32.   Immediate clearing of sufficient acreage for twelve holdings and initial clearing of one village site are priority tasks. If mechanical clearing is used road work will also be necessary. A temporary camp for men employed on clearance will be needed.

33.   A wells team is in the district and a well is to be sunk at Gajale. The importance of water from the very start cannot be overstressed. A well should be sunk in the proposed village area and a dam should be built in the Atumbo River.

34.   The demonstration holding and the assistant's compound should be established or at least well on the way to completion before the arrival of the first settlers.

35.   While work is proceeding to prepare the site, arrangements to inform the overcrowded areas of the scheme and selection of settlers must be made.

36.   Depending, possibly upon the support the scheme receives, a decision must be made with regard to transport. In Uganda transport of settlers to the Kigezi scheme cost £11,395 out of a total expenditure of £18,117 in the first four years.* At Shendam it "has been found that transport is vital to the success of the scheme" and while settlers move on foot, their belongings are carried by lorry.†

37.   The DH and the VH's involved should be taken to Daudawa to see a scheme in action. Differences in detail would have to be explained. The VH Gajale is a young man with primary education.

Conclusion

38.   A settlement scheme as envisaged in this report would necessitate considerable expenditure which might be a reasonable demand on the resources of the Development Board. The alternative to expenditure is simply to mark the area as an agricultural reserve. But one can scarcely expect settlers to adopt mixed farming, farm larger acreages, or live in model compounds unless the inducement of credit is offered. Credit facilities are the best way to increase the yield standards of the average peasant farmer. This does not mean that spoon-feeding (as perhaps has been the case at Daudawa) is desirable. By enforcing strict agreements repayment of credit should be swift. By establishing representative local government alongside the scheme, the settlers should learn that not only are they better off than before but that they are largely the designers of their own fate.

39.   The area is one of the few virgin bush areas left in the province. The need for careful administration of the agricultural and forest resources in so densely populated a province is obvious. The Kiru scheme could become the scene of high productivity, soil conserva-

tion, model farming, and living in a well-ordered community. But it will require imagination by the initiators, enthusiasm by the settlers, and a fund of good will on all sides.

Kibiya
20 Jan 52

* J. W. Purseglove, "Re-settlement in Kigezi, Uganda," *Journal of African Administration*, III (Jan., 1951).
† E. O. W. Hunt, *An Experiment in Resettlement* (Kaduna: Government Printer, 1951).

Monthly Report: Southern Touring Area, Kano Division

General

Resthouses

Without exception all resthouses are in need of log books. Most of the existing books date back to the early twenties and appear to have barely escaped destruction by fire.

2. Sanctions for the payment of caretakers are still not through in Karaye, Rano, and Tudun Wada districts. The caretakers at Tudun Wada and Karaye have not been paid since April, 1951. DH's do not seem to have been active in worrying the NA, and it appears that unless some steps are taken at the center a lapse may become a habit.

Rano District

Administration

3. The main task of the month has been the establishment of local government. All village councils have held their first meetings and it is hoped that the district council will meet in February. On the whole council members have shown some appreciation of what it all means. It is interesting that despite the proximity of Dawakin Kudu,[1] even in the northern part of the district few if any had heard of local government before. One or two lapses have occurred, one VH believing the first meeting to be the signal for raising a levy of 6d., another substituting his *yara*[2] for the elected representatives, and most meetings have been simply a listing of demands. Heading the list are wells, permission to cut trees, and poison for monkeys.

4. Development in the districts will inevitably lead to the disclosure of boundary anomalies. An important one was made obvious by the establishment of village councils. The northern boundary with Dawakin Kudu is the river Challawa with two exceptions. One of these is unfortunate from an administrative point of view. A narrow bridge-

---

1. The first district to have a council.
2. Hangers-on, literally "boys."

head from Dawaki reaches six miles into Rano. There are no villages of importance but it divides two big Rano towns, Barkun and Kumurya. The road connecting these is maintained by Rano. As there are no markets in the bit of Dawaki and, as for much of the year, the river cuts if off from the parent district, the people use the amenities of Rano without in any way contributing to their management. It would seem that a boundary revision is required.

5. The VH's of Nariya and Faram both live in Kibiya. Their respective villages border the district headquarters. The VH Nariya is the son, and the VH Faram the brother, of the VH Kibiya. The family is a wealthy one and occupies some of the best houses in the town. The VH Nariya together with a brother, the scribe of VH Kibiya (and of course his son), have been involved in an assault case in which the woman sanitary inspector was the complainant. The family tends to throw its weight about and it seems desirable that these two VH's should be made to live in their own villages.

6. Work on the new office has begun. Demolition, leveling, and foundation trenches are completed.

Agriculture

7. Sixteen hundred farmers in four village areas are to receive free fertilizer. Two assistants have been posted but have not yet arrived. Farmers will be chosen for the free issue as far as possible from among those who farm close to roads and tracks, particularly those leading to the main markets.

8. There is some excellent dry-season farming along the river Gindawa. For fifteen miles there is almost an unbroken succession of mango trees, bananas, sugar cane, rice, onions, and wheat. A few farmers are growing carrots. The standard of farms is high and their owners are prepared to do road work to find the price of manure. The DH is eager to introduce more European-type vegetables.

Education

9. A football field has been cleared outside Kibiya and the first game has been played. It seems a pity that the Education Department allowed four crossbars and two uprights, instead of the reverse, to be sent out. The resulting goals are monstrous for small boys.

10. One of the Kibiya schoolrooms was to be replaced this year. The site is there with the existing cement floor, but so far nothing has been done. The two classes have to use the one surviving classroom and the small hut which is the headmaster's office.

11. A competition between the three schools in the district has re-

vealed standards far lower than would the usual inspection. At Rurum for example, only two boys in Class 2 were capable of reading a single word from an unseen passage in a supplementary reader for Class 1. In none of the classes were boys able to repeat in their own words what they had just read.

12.   Low standards at Rurum may be due to the headmaster's defective eyesight. He has paid no attention to frequent advice to have his eyes tested and obtain spectacles. He can read only with difficulty, holding the book an inch or two from his face. He also suffers from the unfortunate complaint of being cross-eyed. With his physical disabilities he is unable to teach or supervise properly. As touring officers have gone unheeded, perhaps his department could insist on his seeking attention.

13.   With three schools the expansion of one of them to a four-class school at an early date is desirable. Of the three, the one-class school at Bunkure is situated in much the most important town with respect to size, wealth, and educational demand.

Markets

14.   It has been agreed that the site of Kibiya market should be changed. The VH and elders have chosen a site only a few yards away, inside the town walls and the same waterlogged area. Told to look outside the walls they chose a site by the east gate. This site is also badly flooded during the rains. Apart from the VH and his cronies villagers favor the north gate. The VH's house is close to the east gate, and with only one exception all the ward heads live in the east ward, hence their choice. The site outside the north gate is unfarmed, remains dry alongside the Kibiya-Rano road, which in future will be the route to Kano. It is strongly recommended that the market be moved to this site.

15.   The slaughter slab at Rano market needs repair. This is a very large market, attracting thousands every Friday, and many cattle are killed.

Resthouses

16.   Only Kibiya RH is being maintained. The RH at Rano is habitable in the dry season. It is well situated for *jangali* touring and as a night stop for those making the journey from Kano to Riruwe by car. At present with two government officers in the district it is being used and when the Rano-Chiromawa road is begun will be a suitable place for the officer in charge to stay. It is therefore suggested that the allocation for Kibiya RH be split to allow both to be repaired before the wet season.

Town layouts

17. A separate report on Taria village has been submitted.
18. Rurum requires a new layout away from the huge rock which dominates the town. There is, however, little desire to move although all complain bitterly about the hardships they suffer in the rains.
19. Many villages in Rano are built upon granite rock bed. For this reason the digging of *salgas*[3] is extremely difficult. The old insanitary habits prevail. If the NA were to purchase an Oka drill a complete village could be provided with latrines in a few days. The drill is the product of the Rockefeller Research Institute and is used extensively in the Middle East to provide what is known as the "Rockefeller latrine."

Kiru District

Land settlement

20. A survey of an area northeast of Gajale has been conducted during the month with the object of finding a suitable area for a land settlement scheme.

Tin mining

21. The old workings southwest of Gajale are again in use. About sixty tributers are living in the camp. Most of them are Kano men. The tin is bought every Friday by a Mr. Gillies who drives up from Zaria Province.

Water supplies

22. A Rural Water Supplies team is working in the district.

Tudun Wada District

Administration

23. Owing to the distance of this district from Kano and its own peculiar geography, it seems in every way desirable that the DH should have a car. He needs one more than any other DH, but up to the present his request for an advance has been refused. He tours a great deal keeping a useful gazetteer of his district. The journey to Riruwe is increasingly difficult to make on horseback as there are no longer any villages in which to pass the night and the RH at Yaryasa has been abandoned.
24. The senior scribe has applied for an advance to obtain dentures. His teeth are in poor shape and he is frequently ill. His work suffers as

3. Deep pit latrines.

a consequence. The application was made over eight months ago and has been completely ignored in what seems to be the customary way with Tudun Wada affairs. I consider the matter should be taken up.

25.   The DH was informed last year that it was intended to open a district council in November, 1951. He was asked to proceed with the preliminary propaganda. Naturally enough the failure to keep the promise has added to the general frustration felt in this district.

26.   A revision of the salary of the VH Karefa has been requested. He receives 26/3d. a month. He has been a VH for six years and has 2,628 taxpayers in his village area, which is by far the largest in the district and growing steadily. The VH is one of the lowest paid. This matter has been raised before by both touring officers and the DH.

Agriculture

27.   The price offered at the groundnut buying stations in Tudun Wada was £30 per ton. This is locally regarded too low and most farmers transport their nuts to the railway at Dan Gora.

Town layouts

28.   Surveyors have this month completed the layouts for several villages in the district, and for Tudun Wada itself.

Kibiya
4 Feb 52

Report on Tarai Village

D.O.

In accordance with your instructions I visited Tarai on the sixth of January, inspected the village, and held a meeting with its inhabitants.
2. There is no doubt that Tarai needs opening up. It is cramped into a small area beneath a rocky hill, surrounded by a deep moat, and cut into sections by long and unusually deep borrow pits. The buildings literally rise out of these pits. Few streets are more than three feet wide and the space between huts is often less than a foot. Owing to the lack of space within compounds and the difficulty of easy access to the farms, due to the wall and moat, stockpiling of refuse and night soil is common in the few available public places. Flies are abundant, and meat on sale was completely hidden by the flies settled upon it.
3. Facts concerning a compound chosen at random are:

(i) The area was impossible to measure but was not more than 1,000 sq. ft.
(ii) Number of families: 6
(iii) Total persons: 29
(iv) Number of huts: 13
(v) Number of shelters: 3
(vi) Number of corn bins: 6
(vii) The compound had the usual complement of fowls, goats, and donkeys. Despite the fact that the huts were less than three feet apart somebody was spinning. There were two trees and a well.

4. On health grounds Tarai should be condemned. Apart from the risk of infection (an outbreak of cerebral spinal meningitis would be disastrous), the village boasts an unusually high birth rate. This is attributed to the efficacious waters (a place less like a spa would be hard to find), but is probably due to the overcrowded conditions. Some children are, I am told, the result of incest.
5. The villagers showed intelligent appreciation of the proposal to change their abode. Historically the overcrowding has arisen from the need for protection, the peculiar siting of the town, and the reputation of its waters. A small attempt to extend the town to the south with well laid out compounds has been begun, but even here the old habits

linger and compounds are unnecessarily small. The villagers agree to move on the condition that they receive some financial compensation. It was made clear to them that the NA will not build a complete new village.

6.   I strongly recommend that Tarai be cleared and demolished. The huge pits could be filled with the rubble. The new ward could be retained and made the basis of a new layout. The terrain is suitable.

7.   Financial assistance is important. However much one argues that fire and disease would bring havoc Tarai has experienced neither. Added to which the high birth rate is regarded as proof of "teeming" good health. Without compensation it might be dangerous to try and force a move which is the DH's plan. The discomfort of overcrowding is sufficient to make the villagers want to move, but is not enough to get them to do so.

8.   Comments of previous touring officers as recorded in the District Note Book are attached.

Kibiya
9 Jan 52

Town is in a disgusting state. Houses far too close to each other, the streets merely passages with room for only two people to pass. The wells were surrounded with green slime and the huge pits which divide the town into quarters were filled with the most noisome rubbish as was the moat which surrounds the town. The DH has a new site to the north of the town and will try and get a surveyor out from Kano.

J.B.
15/4/45

Still in a horrible state!

D.H.L.M.
18/12/46

This town is a disgrace to the Administration of this Province. Many villages I have seen are untidy, badly laid out, and dirty, but Tarai is in a class by itself. The death rate is high in the village and the reasons are not difficult to see. Extreme measures must be taken before it becomes a cesspit of disease and squalor unsurpassed in the whole of the North of Nigeria. It is a first rate case for the model layouts one hears so much about. The town carries on a flourishing weaving and dyeing industry and the VH is better than most—but is fighting a losing battle in the village against the inroads of slime and filth.

A.D.H.P.
8/5/48

Mr. Paterson's remarks, unfortunately, still largely true. Town has been opened up to a very minor degree, but the vast majority of the people refuse to adopt the only solution to the present congestion, which is to move out to the new area—only a handful have done so. Pressed to give reasons, the reluctant majority said they would move if the NA built houses for them on the new site. A small market has been opened near the latter. The town boasts an excellent water supply—its waters are widely reputed to be efficacious in cases of barrenness in women, people coming from as far afield as Katsina to purchase. None of the compounds inspected had the regulation latrine, for which there is hardly room amongst the jumble of huts. VH ordered to carry out a drive on this. Village remains the biggest fire and disease hazard in the Province.

T.B.R.
7/3/51

Monthly Report: Southern Touring
Area, Kano Division

General

Resthouses

All sanctions have now been issued and the caretakers have had their arrears of pay made good.

Rano District

Administration

2. All village councils have held their first meetings. An agenda for the district council meeting has been compiled from the village council minute books. It was hoped that the council would meet in February but this has not proved possible due to the absence of the Ciroma in Kaduna.[1] In the district considerable disappointment has been expressed at the delay especially as there is not much left of the building season and it was intended to put work in hand before the rains.

3. £30 has been allocated to the district for RH maintenance, and it is intended to divide this sum between Kibiya and Rano RH's. At Kibiya the resthouse, *bayan gida*,[2] kitchen, servants' quarters, and stable have been thatched.

Communications

4. Work on the Kibiya-Rano road continues. The sense of this is not well understood in the district. Many consider it an *aikin bansa*.[3] The DH and VH's have been informed of the overall roads policy, and the

1. To attend the meeting of the Northern House of Assembly. It was unthinkable that a new district council could meet without the presence of the NA official responsible for the districts and local government. This was the beginning of a great slowdown in NA work. I believe we were mistaken and should have been less sensitive to protocol, allowed things to forge ahead, and broadened thereby the basis of the elite.
2. Latrine.
3. Useless work. Local opinion favored expenditure on the existing road to Kano. We were planning for the future, making a link to the new Trunk Road A1, the trace of which had not even been cut.

DH at least will welcome a good road to Rano, which he visits every Friday.

5. The condition of other roads is very poor and apart from making river beds passable little work has been done.

6. Two meetings have been held of all farmers who farm the borders of the Kibiya-Rano road. The purpose of the road was explained and also the NA Soil Conservation Order. The distance to be left between the side of the road and edge of a farm was demonstrated. It is hoped to hedge this road during the rains and to bridge the ditches where important bush tracks cross them.

Town layouts

7. Work on evacuating Tarai has begun. As compensation is assessed more volunteers come forward requesting new plots and demolition of their existing compounds. It seems likely that the operation will have to be spread over two building seasons. Once the new village begins to appear it is anticipated that more will want to move out.

Tudun Wada District

Administration

8. The DH has been extremely active in organizing labor for tsetse clearance in the Riruwe area. Doguwar Giginya is a control point in the operation and will house seven hundred laborers until camps are built. In a whirlwind tour the DH made the necessary arrangements and put the local population in the picture.

9. Tudun Wada resthouse has been completely repaired.

10. Riruwe resthouse is being repaired. £20 has been allocated and will be sufficient to thatch and provide a cement floor.

11. The NCO and six NA police stationed at Riruwe were smart and efficient when inspected. The mining companies, however, have a poor opinion of their ability to deal with thieving. I was told that they only put on uniform on Saturday when they attend the weekly pay-out by the companies.

12. The police barracks were built in May, 1951, but have never been occupied. They are already riddled with termites and need repair before they can be occupied.

13. The barracks consist of a charge office, seven living quarters, and four latrines. All buildings are badly built, the mud walls half the usual width. At current local prices £50 would have built the lot. The DH has refused to certify the work of the contractor as satisfactory, but I understand the contractor has been paid. Apart from low standards of construction kitchens have not been provided and the well

which was part of the contract has not been sunk. A court of inquiry is indicated.[4]

14. The police live in quarters provided by the companies. The Manager of Tin and Columbite intends to evict them as he requires the camp they are using.

15. The police have one bicycle between them. As the barracks has been sited several miles away from Riruwe and from the major tin workings a second and possibly a third cycle will be needed.

Agriculture

16. Sugar manufacture is important at Birji and Maraku. Competition from Anchau in Zaria is slowly killing Maraku as a sugar market. The village is on high ground surrounded by *fadama*[5] on which far more cane could be, and once was, grown. The finished product is superior in color and purity to that made in Kiru and Karaye.

17. Cotton does well in the south of the district. A cotton market at Doguwar Giginya would attract plenty of trade.

18. There is ample land in the district for settlement. Already settlers move in from Zaria and the present tsetse clearance campaign will open up a lot of land.

Communications

19. The Rano–Tudun Wada road is not one of the best but little used by traffic.

20. The Tudun Wada–Riruwe road is just passable.

21. From the Zenabi junction all roads in the Riruwe area are maintained by the mining companies. They are all season and outshine the rest of the roads in the province. The cost of maintenance is £40 per mile. Culverts are either planking or oil drums. Larger rivers are bridged with concrete culverts. Each company keeps a well-supervised gang permanently at work on its section of roads.

Education

22. Tudun Wada school is being repaired.

23. When future development of educational facilities in this district is considered Doguwar Giginya in the south and Karefa in the north are the most suitable sites for schools.

Legal

24. The *alkali* at Riruwe is young and well educated. He is literate in English and I found him reading a copy of the *Islamic Review*. He seems worthy of a more important court.

4. *Dan Kade* was a good DH. He would be held responsible for the condition of the barracks but was given no control over their construction, something organized in Kano and no doubt involving corrupt arrangements with the contractor.
5. Marsh.

25. The courthouse is far from adequate. There is nowhere to store records or safeguard cash. When funds permit a permanent building incorporating an office for the VH, who has more need for this than the average VH, should be provided, with a safe that can be used by both the court and the DH. Meanwhile a cupboard would help.

26. The prison is large and adequate although short of ventilation in the cells.

27. The *alkali* is allowed to issue rail warrants for warders and prisoners traveling to Kano via the Bauchi Light from Kudaru. He cannot do so for his messengers, who take court fees and fines into the treasury. His request to be allowed one warrant a month seems reasonable.

28. Cases during the months of December and January were:

Assault	11
Theft	6
Statutory	1
Divorce	3
Probate	3

29. It would appear from the records that Riruwe was a law-abiding community. According to expatriate miners, a Yoruba storekeeper, and my messenger this is far from true. There is a great deal of drinking and gambling. Tin-thieving is common. The *alkali* admits that he is afraid to use his powers within the mining camps lest he antagonize the Europeans. I have suggested that he and the VH concentrate on cleaning up the village and market where much of the gambling takes place.

30. Few local men are involved in mining. There is little farming. Most of the inhabitants are traders, living on the mining community and helping them to lose their pay packets in an orgy of gambling which starts midday Saturday and dies out during Monday. Some local men are also agents for tin thieves. Mining camps inevitably lead to a lowering of standards and the community is very mixed. The *alkali* seems genuinely perturbed by the state of affairs but needs much more encouragement if he is to be instrumental in clearing it up.

Medical

31. The dispensary at Riruwe is well run but the dispenser is working under difficulties. His record books are finished and a drug indent is unsupplied. The huts for in-patients are dilapidated and have not been repaired since 1950. His own quarters are in a similar condition. Miners are not slow to point out that the government dispensary falls below the standards required by labor regulations for mining camps.

32. The Sleeping Sickness Service dispenser at Riruwe has only attended eight cases this year, of whom two have run away.

33. The SSS dispensary at Dadin Kowa is in good repair. Attendances are higher than at Riruwe.

34. At both Riruwe and Dadin Kowa in-patients provide their own food. Mining employees are given chop money when sick at rates ranging from 3/6 to 6/– a week according to the company. Others receive 2d. a day from the district imprest. This is a long-standing arrangement. The difference between the NA patient and the mining patient's treatment naturally causes problems.

Markets

35. Doguwar Giginya market is large and prosperous, attracting a lot of Zaria customers. The range of goods is unusually wide. The market is attracting settlement.

Mining

36. A report on taxation problems in the minesfield will be submitted separately.

37. Tin and Columbite, Gold and Base Metals, and Mineral Research Syndicate are the major companies working Riruwe. There are several private miners. MRS are extending their activities to Zenabi and Yelwa. £250,000 will be spent in the neighborhood in the next two years by this company.

38. Labor is short and all companies complain. Any man sacked finds work within a day or so with another company. Labor comes from the seasonal migration of youths from French territory in the dry season, from Fulani herdsmen in the rains, and from pagans from the Plateau when work around Jos is not available. Nearly all labor is therefore seasonal and seldom stays for more than a few weeks. Managements complain that the turnover in labor makes conformation with the labor regulations both expensive and difficult.

39. Tin-thieving is common but so much part and parcel of the mining community that government can hardly be accused. The companies are very bitter about the private miners in this respect.

40. Local managers get along but there is little co-operation between the companies as such. For example there is not a good map of the whole area although all leases are well surveyed. Various rates paid for food and timber cause unnecessary price fluctuations.

41. Mining camps are generally well kept and clean if not obeying the law to the letter. A sanitary inspector is needed for the mining area.

Town layouts

42. Owing to the large influx for the tsetse campaign I have agreed with the DH that work on the layout of Doguwar Giginya be postponed.

43. Dadin Kowa, laid out as a model during the Anchau corridor tsetse campaign, does not remain so. The fault lies with the planners. Streets are so wide that inhabitants naturally farm them. Since eight-lane traffic is unlikely for a century or two one can hardly blame them.

44. Two fires in Riruwe recently destroyed twenty-five compounds. The DH does not consider any relief measures necessary.

45. Rectangular mud block building is common in Riruwe. A Yoruba has taught square thatching of a very high standard. Thatchers from Riruwe might be employed to repair the school buildings that are so badly thatched in other parts of the province.

46. Sun-baked mud bricks sell in Riruwe at 25/- per thousand. Builders charge 25/- for laying the same number.

Water supplies

47. Some of the wells sunk prewar as part of the Anchau scheme now need repair. At Dadin Kowa greater depth is necessary as many wells are already drying up.

Tudun Wada
1 Mar 52

District Council Inspection at
Kumbotso—June 1952

A district council was established in Kumbotso District in September, 1949. The district is small and immediately borders Kano city. The annual revenue of the district council has been in the region of £250. There are ten village councils.

The district council

2. Generally the council appears to be functioning at a consistent level which, if not high, appears adequate. Records showed no sign of advance in maturity which might have been expected after several years. However, it is possible that council meetings themselves have much improved in debate and sense of responsibility.

3. The minute book is reasonably well kept with an attempt at orderliness in dating meetings and listing those present. It is quite a full record of proceedings but does not record dissension or arguments. There is no record of work completed etc. A project book exists but has not been used. The use of the sanction register has not been understood. For example the vote of £50 for "building a council chamber" has been entered at the head of a page. The only other entry is £50 for "erection of council chamber." As kept at present this book is merely a waste of time. The imprest was in order.

4. The council seems to have been saddled with a very heavy burden in that with an income of approximately £250 per annum a dam has been built which originally cost £150 and has been a continual drain of funds since. Otherwise three village council chambers have been built, some wells repaired and cement walled, market stalls erected, slaughter slabs laid, hurumi[1] and cattle tracks marked with compensation paid where necessary, and an anti-thieves campaign held.

5. Most of these smaller projects were completed the first year and it is evident that the life of many is already over. The council chambers are all in need of repair, the wells again need cement, the slaughter slabs are broken, and the market stalls down. Obviously recurrent expenditure is necessary but lack of supervision in the first place has landed the council with heavy subsequent expense.

1. Burial grounds.

6. Apart from the anti-thieves campaign, which appears to have been short-lived as only one arrest is recorded, the council has not attempted to discuss matters of importance in the district which are not building projects. It has failed to express local opinion both on purely district matters and on those things where a district council could be an advisory body to the NA.

The village councils

7. The village councils vary in standard but generally have not been working satisfactorily. Not one has held as many meetings as the district council and many have fallen behind badly. Village heads and *wakilai*[2] are thus attending the district council without any preliminary consultation.

8. Minutes show meetings to have been held on the question and answer basis. It goes rather as follows:

VH   "Kai fa, menene shawararku?"
W   "Maganar rigiya."
VH   "To, kai fa. . . ."[3]

There is seldom if ever any discussion, and it is most noticeable that the minutes tend to divide matters hamlet by hamlet. Nothing seems common to the village council area as a whole.

9. Minute books are not well kept. None had a project register at the back. Several are kept in *ajami*.[4] There appears to be no objection to this especially as more councilors are likely to be literate in *ajami* than roman script. In fact the *ajami* minute books were the neatest.

Suggestions for improvement at Kumbotso

10. That the scribe be shown exactly how to keep all his records. This could not have been done properly in the first place. It might be of help if the NA comments were made in red ink.

11. That the council have explained to them at the next meeting the importance of choosing members to inspect work that is being undertaken. This both to check on contractors and afterward to see immediately repairs are required.

12. That village councils be encouraged to meet before every district council and to improve discussion. This applies also to the district council. While the tone is set by the minute formula of "suna rokon

---

2. Elected representatives as opposed to the ex officio council members such as village heads.
3. "You there, what do you want to raise?"
"The matter of a well."
"All right, you there. . . ."
4. Hausa written in Arabic script.

Sarki ya taimake su da . . . ,"[5] any real sense of responsibility will remain latent. The council needs to be shown that it is not just a place in which to tabulate demands.

13. That village councils open project registers at the back of their minute books.

14. That the whole question of the dam be reviewed by the NA. The dam has been constructed with both the object of helping Kumbotso and also of demonstrating the use of dams to other councils. It has, as the first, inevitably been something of an experiment. The breach this year will prove a costly item and it does appear that if the council is to stand on its own feet it must be relieved of a major project which was, perhaps, pushed upon it.

General suggestions

15. Much of the failure of the village councils must be laid at the door of the great delay in the ratification of a council meeting's minutes by the NA. Machinery needs to be much quicker if four meetings a year are to be held. If it is impossible to speed the wheels then two meetings are sufficient. The liaison is too weak between NA and district council.

16. I suggest that in a small district village councils are unnecessary and direct representation to the district council might be more successful. This idea did not meet with the approval of the district head.

17. On the subject of projects which require contractors councils should have the opportunity to consult a list of approved contractors. It might be considered whether a compulsory list be compiled for the use of councils. Contract forms in Hausa would be of use.

18. The Works Department of the NA would perform a useful service if standard specifications for the usual items of expenditure by councils, such as slaughter slabs, well tops, market stalls, etc., could be supplied. The slaughter slabs laid at Kumbotso are far too small and incorrectly drained. A council should have the opportunity to obtain free technical advice from the NA.

19. Generally the council seemed in need both of protection from itself and from bad contractors. This can best be obtained by the central NA organization which, while not spoon-feeding the council, can offer good advisory services in much the way that the Ministries of Health and Town and Country Planning advise English local government authorities.

Kano
17 Jun 52

5. "They beg the Emir to help them with. . . ."

Adult Literacy Campaign
Progress Report

Kano Division

Kano NA

Forty-five centers have been opened and 1,225 pupils enrolled in literacy classes. The centers are grouped into three schemes and ten independent centers.

2. The Dambatta Scheme with twenty centers is working well. M. Maje, the organizer, understands the teaching method and is able to keep instructors up to the mark. He could, however, tour more frequently than he does. Attendance at classes is good and the district head visits regularly. Many village heads are attending classes as pupils.

3. The Ungogo Scheme with five centers is small but working well. The instructors are among the best in the emirate. There is a large number of township laborers among the pupils. M. Inuwa, the organizer, is old and not really suited to the task. He will have to be replaced next year, possibly by the best instructor.

4. The Rano Scheme with ten centers is not satisfactory. M. Abba, the organizer, is below standard and makes no effort at all. He does not correct instructors' mistakes and offers them no assistance. He cannot take a class as competently as many instructors. He should be dismissed as his presence is more of a hinderance than if there were no organizer. One instructor has been dismissed. His replacement is being trained. None of the instructors has really grasped the teaching method and attendances are noticeably low—often less than half. The Sanda class is an exception in this respect. The village head, who is one of the best in the division, is himself attending. The district head did not take much notice of the course held by M. Abubakar Kankiya in August and has not been visiting classes.

5. The independent centers in Bici, Dawakin Tofa, Gabasawa, Gezawa, and Minjibir districts do not receive sufficient supervision. The two Bici instructors are very weak. M. Iliyasu, the senior organizer, has spent a week in Bici giving them extra tuition and taking the classes. The D/Tofa instructors were badly chosen as they do not live

in the villages where centers have been opened. This will be rectified as soon as the present "session" is completed. Meanwhile it has been clearly laid down that instructors must come from the places where they are to teach. The Minjibir instructor has been dismissed for incompetence.

6. Thirty instructors are receiving tuition at Wudil this month. They represent the remaining districts of the emirate, two from each, with the exception of Kiru and Kumbotso who failed to send anyone. Nine of the thirty have been sent home as unsuitable. Those who survive the course will immediately open centers in their home towns. The equipment will be waiting for them.

7. Two organizers are under training at Wudil. One has done quite well but the other is not up to standard and should not be appointed. Mr. Court, who is running the course, will report on the best instructors. These will be potential organizers if it is decided to expand to a full scheme in their districts.

8. Classrooms are being built at the various centers by communal labor with NA assistance in the way of doors and windows. The Dambatta classrooms have now all been completed.

9. The next step in the Kano Emirate campaign should undoubtedly be one of concentration in selected districts such as Gwarzo. It is much easier to supervise one scheme of twenty centers with its own organizer than twenty centers scattered through ten districts. Again, instructors can be trained in their own districts and carefully selected before the course begins. District heads are not, on the whole, qualified to assess the abilities of an instructor. This has been proved by the "wastage" on courses held so far and the number of young boys chosen who are obviously not suitable to teach adults. Some of the instructors dismissed from the Wudil course came unwillingly and were pleased enough to go. Pupils must also be well selected. Many village heads cannot be trusted to do this. At one class I sent home five pupils who had been told to come by the village head under the impression that they were to be my carriers!

Kazaure NA

10. Seventeen attended an instructors' course in early November. Twelve were found suitable and have been trained. Centers are now being opened. The Kazaure organizer, M. Lawan, is quite good but lacks initiative and consequently will need plenty of encouragement. The main difficulty in Kazaure is the scattered pattern of settlement. Apart from the four district towns nearly every village area is made up of small and scattered hamlets where a center is unlikely to be a success.

11.   The aim should be to achieve and maintain a high standard in a few centers rather than attempt expansion.

Northern Division

Gumel NA

12.   Twenty instructors are under training. They seem to have been carefully selected and there are no very young boys among them. M. Aminu, the organizer, is old but energetic and should prove quite good. There is considerable active enthusiasm by the Emir which will help a great deal.

Hadejia NA

13.   Twenty-seven instructors have been trained, five of whom were already teaching at existing centers. The remainder are at present opening centers in their home towns.

14.   M. Aliyu, the organizer, has done well and shown considerable initiative in opening five centers without waiting to be told to do so.

15.   The difficult wet season communications will necessitate the division of centers into two schemes, one north and one south of the river. If a fraction of the energy put into Koranic schools in Hadejia can be found for adult literacy the campaign should be a success.

General

Provincial newspaper

16.   Plans are in hand to produce a provincial newspaper as an insert to *Jakadiya*.[1] It will be printed and published in Zaria. The editor will be attached to the vernacular literature section of the Regional Adult Education Office. In the future it is hoped to produce this paper in the Kano Native Administration Printing Press.

17.   Contributions for the newspaper are being collected by organizers from the various centers and individual pupils.

18.   A competition was held among instructors to choose a name for the newspaper. Some good names were submitted and the popular vote favored *Sodangi*,[2] which is appropriate and very suitable from a journalistic point of view.

Selection and training of personnel

19.   Good organizers and instructors are essential for the success of the campaign. At present several organizers are below standard and

1. A vernacular newspaper especially aimed at graduates of literacy classes.
2. A name which means homelover and friend of all. It used to be given to a child born after the mother's return home after a long absence.

with bad instructors can be weeded out, and the indifferent improved provided refresher courses are held every year, or preferably every six months between sessions. In future the selection of instructors must be made by the central staff from a district head's candidates. Where district schemes are opened this should be easy to do.

20. For organizers the campaign must compete with other departments who all require the best caliber men available. However, character matters far more than academic qualifications, and the better type organizer may well come from the class of men who lacked the opportunity for more than an elementary education. Nepotism and the "jobs for the boys" principle (which now has a political aspect in Kano) have got to be fought. Ruthless dismissal of bad organizers would appear to be the solution. In this respect it must be remembered that organizers' salaries and allowances are refunded to native authorities by government.

Classrooms

21. Both instructors and pupils like to have a classroom and the idea should be encouraged. But consideration must be given to the combination of the adult literacy center with the village council hall. The single English village hall serves for a variety of purposes including parish council meetings. To build a council hall for a possible four meetings each year and then to build other rooms for other purposes is an extravagance that cannot be justified. Where a "multiple purpose" hall is to be built the labor can be supplied communally (as for the classrooms) and district council funds assist with a cement floor, door, and windows. A saving in both central and district funds would be made.

Conclusion

22. Finally it must be reported that there is considerable keenness on the part of many pupils. Where attendance is low the fault usually lies in bad instruction or bad selection of pupils. Teaching problems are bound to occur but I have gained the impression while visiting centers that the campaign is gathering strength and momentum like a snowball. We will have to insure that the organization keeps pace with the pupils.

Kibiya
25 Nov 52

Progress Report on the Adult Literacy Campaign, Zaria Province

Owing to lack of supervision the literacy campaign got out of hand during 1953. There were more classes than could be adequately supervised by the existing staff of organizers, and as a result instructors did not receive as much training as is desirable. Nevertheless progress has been made and detailed plans for the next financial year have been prepared.

2. 2,480 literacy certificates have been awarded to date. During his annual tour the Emir personally presented certificates in every district. The encouragement to all is considerable and I hope that the Emir will continue to do this in future years.

Organizers

3. The organizers have, on the whole, done a creditable job in spite of difficulties. Their reports are good and honest. Unfortunately their claims for allowances are seldom made out with the same attributes, and disciplinary action has been taken against one organizer on this count.

4. From April 1 the staff of organizers will be increased to fourteen. This will allow one organizer in each of the larger districts. Efficiency will be increased as supervision is restricted to a limited area. To avoid paper work and remove the temptation to submit false claims all organizers will receive a monthly allowance of £3 in addition to salary. This consolidated allowance is reimbursable by government. It will replace bicycle allowance, traveling allowance, out-of-pocket expenses for carriers, train and lorry fares. The organizers have accepted the change and the Regional Adult Education Office has approved in principle. Among the obvious advantages is the simplification of budgeting.

Instructors

5. Instructors vary from good to very bad. We still have to put up with some village heads' sons who want a few shillings a month to add to their income as village scribes. When they fail to do their job the VH is unlikely to object. With regular visits by organizers, which we can expect after April, it should be possible to combat this problem,

and I am encouraging a policy of ruthless dismissal of incompetent instructors. The man who is genuinely prepared to help his fellow villagers may not always be a good instructor but he is capable of improvement; the idle parasite is of no use at all and must go.

6. From April the number of classes will be increased to 400. At present there are 277. Eventually we shall need about 650 classes if the province is to be adequately covered. Appendix A shows the distribution of classes. The extra instructors required for the increase in classes are by no means all ex-primary-school boys. The best of them are those who have themselves learned to read and write in an adult literacy class.

7. The principle has now been accepted that whenever possible the instructor should be a native of the village where he instructs. There are surprisingly few villages with no literates at all. Instructors who have to travel any distance to their classes soon fall by the wayside—if they ever leave their own *zaure* during the rains!

8. Many classes have their own building. The NA provides doors and windows and the villagers do the rest. The use of these buildings for other activities such as village council meetings is being encouraged in the hope that one day they will play the part that the village hall does in English rural communities.

Courses

9. During March and April courses for all organizers and all instructors are being held. As far as possible every district is having its own course, thus saving hardship to part-time instructors who naturally do not wish to be away from home for long. During the two-week courses a subsistence allowance of 1/– a day in the districts and 1/3 a day in Zaria is being paid.

10. The missions have been invited to send a limited number of instructors to these courses. The teaching method is suitable for adult classes of religious instruction. Any other sponsored classes may also send instructors for training. This is the best way for the NA to assist other agencies at work in the field of adult literacy.

Distribution of literature

11. A successful stall was a feature of the Zonkwa Agricultural Show on January 23. Apart from the demonstration value of the stall, which with its colored banner and posters was one of the attractions of the show ground, nearly £5 worth of literature was sold. As this sum was made up by the sale of books priced 1*d.* and 2*d.* it represents a considerable volume of business.

12. Touring officers are helping by carrying a supply of suitable books, and my own experience has proved how easy it is to sell them

even in the remotest village. After village meetings in the afternoon I have sometimes sold £1 worth in under twenty minutes. It is difficult to carry enough.

13. Generally, however, the distribution system is lamentably weak. It is, I am convinced, useless to attempt to use the NA channel. Which district office has not got its stock of *Jakadiya* and *Gaskiya ta fi Kwabo*[1] hidden in the cupboard? Traders are needed who will take up distribution as a serious line of business. In the villages a 20 per cent discount is not a bad inducement but the unfortunate village trader has no facilities for either sending money or collecting the books from Gaskiya Corporation. Those who have are too big to be bothered with a mere 20 per cent. I have several small village traders who accept £1 worth of books provided that I take them out to them. The solution will be the provincial book van which we should get during the coming year. It will be able to distribute to traders as well as sell directly.

Postal services

14. Postal services are very poor in the province. This is a serious matter as the encouragement of literacy greatly depends on the facilities for its use. My own experience is that the new literate would rather use his skill to write a letter than to read a book. The very strict regulations of the Posts and Telegraphs Department make it virtually impossible for the average Northerner to open a postal agency. Fluency in English and pan-roofed buildings are rare except among strangers along the railway line. If Hausa is an official language in the Region it seems fair that postal regulations should be available in it, and that the department be able to transact its business in Hausa as well as English. This is a matter which could usefully be discussed at a higher level.

15. District councils might well be encouraged to establish carrier services between districts and the nearest postal agency. More wealthy NA's are able to use messengers but Zaria has no *dogarai* and could ill afford them.

General

16. The most disappointing thing about the campaign in Zaria is the lack of interest displayed by district and village heads. I do not expect much from the older school of VH's but the DH's ought to do more than pay lip service to the instructions of the NA. I have yet to find a DH who could tell me where the classes in his district were and when they meet. Apart from in the visitors' book of the class in the district

1. Vernacular newspapers supposedly for resale in districts.

HQ I have seldom seen a DH's signature. The latest example of indifference occurred this week when the DH Igabi, with no excuse, failed to send instructors to the course arranged for them in Kaduna. The Galadima in Zaria city denied all knowledge of a letter informing him of the course for his instructors until shown it in his own files. The unfortunate instructors in both cases were three days late and had had no previous warning. The regional government is constantly stressing the importance of the literacy campaign. The words of His Honour to the House of Chiefs this month might well be printed and distributed to DH's and senior NA officials. I hope that DHs' responsibilities can be brought home to them when they next gather in Zaria.

17.   With effect from April a government provincial adult education officer and a supervisor will be appointed for the province. When the book van arrives a salesman and a driver will also be appointed. With this central organization and the posting of organizers to districts there is every hope that the campaign will go from strength to strength. It should be possible for the new staff to devote time to the important business of distributing news. The radio should soon be playing a part as well as the vernacular newspapers. There is much to be done and at long last it seems that the province will have the field staff to do it.

Zaria
4 Mar 54

Touring Notes: Kauru District,
Zaria Division

Kauru District has not been thoroughly toured by an administrative officer since 1938. Dr. East paid a visit in 1942 and Mr. McCallum in 1946, but neither was able to see all the tribes and villages. So many things came to light during my tour that I feel it is worthwhile to put up fairly extensive notes including paragraphs on the twelve pagan tribes in the district, and a summary of proposals which are, in my opinion, essential for the future welfare and development of a much neglected area.

2. The district is divided sharply into two. The plain in the north contains the Hausa villages and in the south are grouped twelve tribes in and around the Kauru and Surubu hills. The Gure and Kahugu tribes of Lere District are also in the Kauru hills and much that applies to the Kauru tribes is equally applicable to them. The Kauru hills are mountains of great and varied beauty. The highest peak, Gyshere Hill, is 4,203 feet above the sea level. In the hills are many well-watered and lovely valleys. I gather from the note books that administrative officers in the past, burdened with topees, spine-pads, and breeches, preferred to ride around the hills rather than walk through them. They missed a lot.

3. The welcome I received everywhere, including Kauru town, was pathetic in its magnitude. In the hills, from dawn until long into the night, my *zaure* was full of visitors and I was constantly in receipt of addresses of welcome and letters of gratitude. The friendliness of the people made it extremely easy for me to acquire a lot of information in a short time. My tour in itself, whatever else may come of it, has been a considerable morale booster and has allowed a lot of hot air to be satisfactorily dispersed.

Administration

4. The office is a small mud building outside the DH's house and is adequate. M. Juma'are, the junior scribe, is competent and pleasant. M. Tanko, the senior scribe, has been here for twenty-three years and I feel the time has come for both him and Kauru to have a rest. Previous officers have not been impressed by his ability. He reminds

me of Uriah Heep. I strongly recommend his transfer elsewhere, and, if feasible, the promotion of M. Juma'are.

5. The district council is the best I have seen in the province. The DH is keen and genuinely interested in helping things along. The council chamber boasts a radio set and I am pleased to see that all and sundry are allowed to listen. Several excellent *giginya*[1] bridges have been built with council funds. Elections have been held regularly. I recommend this council for increased financial responsibility.

6. One of the most serious complaints that I received in the pagan area was from the village heads. They seldom receive their salaries, which are small enough as it is, because these are intrusted to the care of their scribes for delivery. The scribes are Hausas and therefore have a higher district status than the pagan village heads. I am in favor of all village heads being called in once a month to collect their salaries, hear the news, be given instructions and so on. Communications are difficult in Kauru and few VH's are wealthy enough to own horse or cycle, but it should be possible to call them in every second month.

7. As mentioned above the village scribes are all Hausa. The excuse that nobody else is capable is no longer tenable. In every tribe I found literates, usually in a higher proportion than one would find in a Hausa village. There are some ex-middle-school boys and several with primary education. Some of the latter were expressly sent to school in order that they become scribes. I found no single thing that upsets the pagans more than this indignity. The situation has been remedied elsewhere (in Zangon Katab and Kachia) and I hope will be done so here without delay. The DH is sympathetic and requires little pushing to make him agree. It is primarily a matter of self-respect, but the non-residency of the Hausa scribes is bad in principle and there are fewer checks on their abuses.

8. Tax collection was complete in the pagan but not in the Hausa villages. There are abuses which can easily be corrected. Collection starts too early in the pagan area, where there are no cash crops. They sell corn to raise money unless they have sufficient of last dry season's earnings with which to pay. Collection has consistently begun before government has approved the rate. The VH's collect the money and take it to Kauru where receipts are written. Individual taxpayers may not get their receipt for many months. Pagans pay tax at a uniform rate. Once cash-crop farming has caught on it should be possible to change this.

9. Everywhere I heard complaints of forced labor, and they have substance. Road work, repair of NA buildings, erection of cotton markets, etc., are by no means always paid for. I have warned all

1. A palm whose timber is termiteproof and therefore much used in building.

concerned and am pursuing particular cases. Unfortunately the peasant does not usually realize that he is entitled to any payment. There is urgent need for the publication of wage rates and the types of work for which payment is made, as distinct from legitimate communal labor.

10. The purchase of corn for the NA famine relief store gives rise to many abuses. I strongly recommend its complete abolition if possible. The NA could buy through contractors or the Mokwa scheme and the extra expense would be well worth the good will gained. In the pagan areas corn is short and the quantity to be sold can be a hardship in itself. The price paid—when received in full—is low. A journey is involved and I found people being kept hanging about for three or four days. Some VH's even extract money in lieu of corn. The deeper I delved the murkier I found the picture.

11. The NA Dog Licensing Order caused considerable discontent among dog-owning tribes. Fortunately I was able to spread the news that the order had been wrongly applied to the districts and was intended only for Zaria and Kaduna urban areas.

12. The Bicycle Licensing Order is causing no trouble. Collection is almost complete. I am convinced that the revenue from cycle licenses will be the *jangali* of the future. No one seems to mind and there even seems to be prestige value attached to the licensing plates. If plates ran out there might be trouble!

13. Two boundary disputes were brought to my notice and the DH would welcome the assistance of an ADO in settling them. The Kitimi require an area in the plains for farming and possible settlement, and there is a dispute between the Kono and Kahugu which involves the district boundary with Lere. In neither case is there a shortage of land. I will attend to the matter when next in the district.

14. The tribes on the east side of the hills complain of the Fulani who move into the area before harvest and whose cattle damage the corn. The DH confirms this. It is difficult to see what can be done. Once the harvest is over the Fulani are welcome, high prices are paid for manure, and everyone enjoys the milk. Possibly a patrol of mounted NA police during the crucial time would help.

15. The district would be a good one in which to encourage co-operatives. The small tribes are a suitable size. The hill people are thrifty by nature, and a good co-operative might help provide cohesion in the disintegrating tribal life. I will try and get an assistant registrar to tour. In the meantime I spoke to the educated young men about the general idea of co-operatives.

16. The resthouse at Kauru is adequate but needs a coat of whitewash. Kwasan resthouse has the finest view I have seen this side of Bamenda. It ought to be resited on the plain, but for the sake of fellow

mountaineers it ought to be retained at all costs. Gyshere resthouse is unusable. It has no roof. An estimate for repairs has been submitted. Kaibi is also unusable but should not be repaired. The village has moved away and the resthouse site has nothing to commend it.

17.   I have written an intelligence summary under secret cover.

Agriculture

18.   There are two cotton markets. I was not impressed with the cotton examiner at Kauru, about whom I received many complaints. He wears a large gown and a turban, is surrounded by *yara*,[2] and seldom dirties his own hands with cotton. At Dandaura the young examiner seems efficient.

19.   It seems important, on principle, that, no matter how small the market, there should be at least two buyers. An element of competition would reduce many abuses in single-buyer markets such as false weights.

20.   Farmers are complaining about the new cotton seed used for the first time last year. The quality of lint is high but the yield has been low. Late planting and poor September rainfall seem to be reasons, and I have so informed village meetings.

21.   Not much tobacco was grown last year as a result of marketing troubles. According to the DH sellers were kept waiting five days before a buyer arrived. He closed the market after two days and many farmers were left with tobacco on their hands. I suspect that the unsold leaf was substandard. It does seem, however, that the Nigerian Tobacco Company has been tactless in this area.

22.   I received a request for a groundnut selling station at Dandaura. I do not think it would be justified at present.

23.   Kaura is infested with monkeys and I recommend that the DH be asked to send someone for training as a poisoner and then be given a stock of poison. If necessary district council funds could pay a small wage to the poisoner. In the meantime the Agriculture Department poisoning team should be sent to the district.

24.   The goats in the hills are of a short-legged variety, but the red Sokoto hide is more common than black or mixtures.

25.   There are no sheep in the hills. Cattle graze in the dry season and goats are plentiful. It seems a suitable area for sheep now that there is less demand for land to cultivate. A present of a small flock to the Kitimi might open up a new source of wealth. Expert advice is required.

26.   Pigs are common in the Ruruma villages. They seem to thrive. I hope to investigate the possibility of a pig farming co-operative. The

2. Servants, hangers-on and other unsavory dependents in practice.

pigs are kept by the younger men, who would, I think, respond. Kaduna would provide a ready market for pork.

27. The Kitimi bee-keep on a large scale, every compound having its hives. They are not able to distinguish a queen.

28. It would be of much help if a production officer could be posted to the area. At present they work in areas where farming techniques are good and production of crops is high. In Kauru there is plenty of land, but most of the farmers are still at subsistence level. A production officer would be able to encourage the introduction of cotton and tobacco and help the hill tribes to adapt their hill experience to the plains. The hills are carefully terraced and there is little erosion. Once on the plain antierosion measures are seldom taken, especially if there are Hausa farms nearby setting a bad example in this respect. A demonstration farm would be of little value, but an officer who won the confidence of the people would be able to achieve much.

Communications

29. The Zaria-Pambeguwa road is getting worse. It is exceptionally bad between Dutsin Wai and Pambeguwa. The reason is the heavy cotton traffic. I suggest that this road, which is being reconstructed to all-season standards, carries more traffic than the Kaduna-Jos road and has a strong claim to be upgraded to Trunk Road A. Once the bridges are completed no traffic will go the long way round, and when the new Kano-Zaria road is finished this will be the quickest Kano-Jos route.

30. The dry-season road from Pambeguwa to Kauru is excellent.

31. There is an urgent need for a road from Kauru southward into the hills. A dry-season road would make all the difference to the prosperity of this area. It would do more to encourage production than any other factor. It would encourage the last hill dwellers to descend to good and plentiful farm land.

32. I suggest the following road plan. The first road should be made from Kauru to Kwore and on to Fadan Ruruma at the foot of the escarpment. The next link should be a continuation of the road which is being made in Lere District from Lere to Gure. This could be continued from Gure to Kono and on to Gyshere. Finally, when possible, the two roads could be linked by a road from Fadan Ruruma to Bital and west of the mountain range to Kabene.

33. The NA has not budgeted for any road development in the district. I realize that funds are not readily available. But given limited funds and the tools I am convinced that roads could be built with communal labor. Supervision by an administrative officer would be advisable to insure that one tribe was not forced to do the lion's share, as often happens in communal work. District council funds are too

small. Tools must be bought and communal labor fed. It might be possible to interest the Production Board in the area as a "settlement area."

34. If there is any prospect of this work going ahead I should like to get a road as far as Kwore this dry season to show the DH and people that we mean business. The importance of roads cannot be denied, and in Kauru they would provide both a stimulant to settlement and production and also help consolidate settlement in villages rather than on haphazard farms as at present.

Education

35. There is one two-class junior primary school in Kauru. There is an SIM[3] two-class primary at Kabene. Kauru is the worst-served district in the province by both NA and voluntary agencies.

36. The Kauru school is below standard. The DH is anxious that a teacher who can teach English be found. Without English the children are denied opportunity to continue to senior primary school. Although the classes are II and IV, I found them following the I and III syllabus.

37. The SIM school at Kabene was closed. I was unable to judge the standard, but there is only one classroom.

38. There is no mission school at Kwasam. The provincial education officer has one on his records. I trust no grant is being paid!

39. Kauru should certainly be given next year's community schools.[4] I explained the idea to the DH and at village meetings and the response everywhere was excellent. For the small tribes and varied religions the community school scheme is well suited. I suggest three schools: at Fadan Ruruma for the Ruruma, Rumaiya, and Kaibi; at Kono for the Kono, Dwingi, Kitimi, and Kinuku; and at Gyshere for the Surubu, Kurama, Risjiwa, Binawa, and Kiballo. These three schools are essential. It would be most unjust to increase facilities elsewhere before Kauru obtained the minimum. For example Lere, a neighboring and similar district, has five NA schools. With three schools in the hill area, the Kauru school could be kept exclusively for the Hausa villages in the north.

40. I found several boys in the hills with full primary education which they have obtained by much effort in either Plateau Province NA schools or at the SIM senior primary at Gure. But after primary education they are stuck; the mission offers nothing more, and Plateau

---

3. Sudan Interior Mission, an evangelical church union.
4. An imaginative idea of an excellent education officer. The NA staffed and supported the school if the community built it by its own efforts.

finds them out and sends them back to Zaria. The PEO has kindly agreed to take one boy into the middle school.[5] Another will start training at Wusasa as a nurse in March, and a third is going into the Nigeria Police. It is most fortunate that I have received so much co-operation in doing something for these boys. The area would provide recruits of a high standard for the army—if only some one will go and tell them about it.

41. The twelve adult literacy classes are doing well and will be increased to twenty-five in April. An organizer is to be appointed from the existing instructors, and I have recommended M. Bagobiri (a Ruruma). He is excellent material and easily the best instructor. The appointment of a pagan will do much toward increasing the good will of the NA.[6]

Forestry

42. Throughout the district I received many complaints about the forest assistant. I informed the Emir and asked him to warn the assistant. There is so much ignorance of forest regulations that abuse is easy.

43. One problem concerns farmers opening up new land. The hill tribes are coming down from the hills and the Hausa are enlarging cotton farms. They need to clear the bush. The Provincial Forestry Officer might issue instructions about new farms and clearing.

44. In consultation with the PFO I intend to produce a broadsheet on forest regulations for use in adult literacy classes.

45. Kauru has large forests of *giginya*. I had never before realized what an excellent antierosion factor *giginya* can be. There are no bad gullies at the foot of the hills where *giginya* are growing, although common elsewhere. I understand that tsetse cannot breed under fully grown *giginya*, which provides insufficient shade and prohibits undergrowth. If this is so, *giginya* would be the solution to those areas where antitsetse clearing has resulted in gully erosion.

46. There are many locust bean trees in the hills.

5. He eventually graduated from Ahmadu Bello University and entered the Nigerian Foreign Service.
6. Getting him appointed was really difficult. He became the first non-Hausa on the payroll of the NA except as a village scribe or policeman. To call Bagobiri a pagan is unfair. He was an earnest evangelical Christian, and one of the finest men I ever met. He eventually became the confidant of the DH, much to the latter's surprise, although he was honest enough to admit it. Bagobiri did an enormous amount for the district, his loyalties often torn. The strain on this unusually honest and conscientious man was such that he became mentally ill. Whereas a Hausa official would have been given time to recover, Bagobiri was rapidly dismissed, to the annoyance of the DH. He happily recovered, but his influence for good was lost to the NA which had treated him so shabbily.

Judicial

47. The *alkali's* court is not busy. The books were in order but poorly kept and I was not impressed by the mufti.

48. There are two pagan courts at Kwasam and Gyshere. In 1953 the former tried eighteen cases and the latter seventeen. They are obviously not functioning properly, and matrimonial disputes, of which there must be many, are settled by village heads. The two courts share a scribe, needless to say a Hausa Moslem, who lives in Kauru and visits the courts when he feels like it and never during the rains. He is not impressive and his records are badly kept. His position is such that he tends to overrule court members. I heard rumors, unsubstantiated, that he sometimes heard cases himself. As with the village scribes, the hill peoples want their own court scribe.

49. I suggest that the scribe be transferred to an *alkali's* court when a vacancy occurs and two local men appointed as scribes to the two pagan courts. They should be part-time appointments. The present man gets a full-time salary for an average of eight days' work a year. The court books should be regularly inspected by the DH and taken into Zaria by the *alkali's* mufti when necessary.

50. The Kwasam courthouse should be rebuilt in the plain and not in the old town. The present type of building, a large round hut, is unsuitable. The custom of the people is to hear cases in public and this has many advantages. A three-sided shelter is all that is required.

51. I received complaints about the enforcement of the *iddah* rule[7] from the Surubu, Rishiwa, and Kaibi. The DH tells me that this causes a lot of trouble and he would like a firm ruling one way or the other. The problem does not concern all tribes. The Ruruma have their own form of *iddah* and the Kono, as in most things, have a law to themselves about which it is difficult to obtain information. But they never complain. Marriage by theft is common among the Surubu. Expert advice is needed on this problem which concerns all southern Zaria.

52. The lockup has no compound or sanitation and is badly ventilated.

53. There are two NA policemen. I recommend an increase to three, and if possible to four. Gyshere market is apt to be a trouble spot, and market brawls have a tendency to become tribal. During the dry season police are useful at cotton markets.

---

7. The Moslem law which prohibits a woman from remarrying until three months have elapsed from the date of her divorce. The purpose is to determine whether or not she is pregnant. Divorce is often consequent to adultery but the rule insures legal custody of any child conceived to the former husband. The rule had been applied by the Emir to some of the pagan tribes as well, but was not clear whether to all.

Medical

54. I was most impressed by Kauru dispensary, which has recently been taken over by the NA. I heard no complaints. Both NA and SSS dispensers seem competent.

55. At Gyshere things are far from happy. I am not sure who complains most—the people about the dispenser or the dispenser about the people! Faults are on both sides. The people are reluctant to stay as in-patients and do not co-operate in the sleeping sickness surveys. On the other hand there is little doubt but that medicine is sold and that the dispenser is tactless. At all village meetings I explained that a dispenser is trained to do his job and that if a patient refuses to do as he is told it is his own fault if he doesn't recover. I also stressed the need for continuation with treatment even after apparent recovery and the importance of annual surveys for sleeping sickness.

56. Gyshere is seldom visited by an MO. The dispenser has been here three years and SSS work is suffering. There is a local man, a Kono, who is the SSS dispenser at Rigachikum. I suggest that an interposting be arranged. In any case M. Tanimu should go. No progress will be made while he is here, whereas in a Hausa area he could probably do a good job of work.

57. The dispensary is infested with termites.

58. Drug supplies are sent to Kauru by lorry and there await carriers to Gyshere. This takes weeks as no funds are provided. I suggest that during the dry season drugs are left with the VH at Garun Kurama. This would reduce the trek from thirty-six to sixteen miles and more Gyshere people pass through Garu than Kauru.

59. Everywhere, despite the complaints about the existing dispensary, villagers asked for more. In point of fact they are not badly off. Communications are, however, difficult in the wet season, and I suggest that when funds are available a dispensary be built in the Ruruma area. This would complete the needs of the district.

60. Malnutrition is common among the hill peoples. I noticed a high proportion of goiter and many seemed to suffer from a throat condition that gives them a chronic hoarse voice.

61. Kauru shares a sanitary inspector with other districts. Would it be possible to form a vaccination team to operate in the same group of districts? Very few children have been vaccinated. A good team would be able to get around all of the districts without their own sanitary inspection in a year.

Missions

62. There are no missions in Kauru but several classes of religious instruction have been established from the SIM at Gure and the

Seventh-day Adventists at Jengre. There is one junior primary school at Kabene. The missions have not had much success. The young men resent the fact that they are not helped when they want to enter NA or government schools for higher education, and those who are employed by the missions earn very low wages.

Minerals

63. Prospecting has been going on in the neighborhood of Gyshere and Kono. There is tin at Zamfur. Before any leases are granted the problem of settlement should be carefully considered. Although there is no actual shortage of land there is a preference to farm as close as possible to the old hill villages.

Water supplies

64. When possible a wells team should come to the district. The careful siting of a well can make a big difference to the settlement of the area.

65. There are many streams and excellent dam sites. A few well-placed dams should solve what few water problems exist.

Kauru hill tribes

66. There has been a tendency in the past to treat the tribes as variations on a common theme. I doubt the wisdom of this. It seemed to me that almost certainly the tribes on the eastern and western slopes have different origins. Languages and building techniques are different. Fortunately nobody has ever suggested a paramount chief. The important thing, however, is the stage the tribes have now reached rather than speculation about their origin. Generally it should be remembered that most of the tribes were fighting one another within living memory and still retain considerable independence and pride.

The Rumaiya

67. With very few exceptions all the tribe has moved to the plain. The main village, Galadimawa, has completely settled—the *Sarkin Dutse*[8] moving down last year. He is reputed to be a hundred, and looks twice that age! Settlement has been haphazard and homes are scattered. The VH of Galadimawa is the senior chief of the tribe and seems to have control but the subchief of Garmadi is unhelpful and not respected. Wells are needed around which settlement can be planned.

68. The Rumaiya have been farming cotton for years but still have to

8. "King of the hills," tribal priest.

call in Hausa women to pick it. All are heavy smokers, the girls starting well before puberty. It should be possible to encourage the planting of tobacco as a cash crop.

69. The out-station of Gure mission has been closed, but there are several literates, including one or two boys who attended school at Wusasa.[9]

70. Of all the tribes the Rumaiya seem the most "lost" and consolation in beer-drinking is the main dry-season occupation of the men. The younger generation is not strong enough to exercise the influence it does elsewhere.

The Ruruma

71. The main village, Kwasam, is in the hills, but there is a new village below where many of the younger men are building homes. The subvillages of Fagen Rawa and Fadan Ruruma are also on the plain. The latter has consolidated around a cement-lined well. The chief remains in Kwasam, where resthouse, courthouse, and a church are situated.

72. Cash-crop farming is on a small scale. The younger men keep pigs, which seem to thrive.

73. The tribe are noted builders. Their own houses are built of stone and there are many dry stone walls reminiscent of the Lake District.

74. The young men travel far and wide in the dry season in groups of three or four seeking work as builders. As a result, combined with mission influence, there are considerable enlightenment and many literates. The tribe seems well integrated. The young men are persuading their elders to move from the old town. The Chief of Fadan Ruruma is a keen young fellow and the tribal chief far from old. The Chief of Fagen Rawa seems without influence, and might usefully be retired.

75. Much could be done in the way of community development among the Ruruma once they are given a sense of self-respect and a lead. A well at Fagen Rawa and another at Sabon Garin Kwasam might assist settlement. The courthouse should be moved to the plain and Fadan Ruruma made the terminal point of the access road from Kauru.

The Kitimi

76. The Kitimi live right in the center of the hills in an extremely beautiful series of valleys. These are well watered and full of locust bean trees. Farms are carefully terraced. Some farm in the plain, but they are seven miles away on difficult paths. An area needs to be

9. A Church Missionary Society mission station on the outskirts of Zaria.

demarcated for them as they suffer at the hands of the Ruruma who are more strongly established on the plain.

77. With their careful techniques and thrifty habits I think there is enough land in the hills to provide them with food but not cash crops. The area seems ideal for sheep, but whether this would merely create other problems is a matter for expert advice. I cannot see the Kitimi moving away yet awhile.

78. The chief is a Moslem and many have followed his lead. As a result some of the older men cling to the traditional way of life even more persistently than elsewhere.

The Kono

79. Of all the tribes the Kono seem most virile. They have a reputation for being troublesome, and in the past were the most renowned warriors. They were subdued by the 1907 patrol. They live on the edge of the hills overlooking Lere District. Many live in the old villages which are only a ten-minute climb from the plain, but more and more are settling on the plain. Cement-lined wells have kept the villages together. Physically the Kono stand out. They appear better nourished, are tall, and well built. They are very independent and have been very selective in the adoption of either Islamic or Western ideas.

80. Cash crops are grown on a small scale. Fishing is a dry-season pastime and they make good nets. Like the Ruruma they build well. Personally I think they build better, and I have never stayed in a better *zaure*. Sun-dried bricks are used, a skill acquired from the mission at Gure.

81. There are many literates, and several boys have completed senior primary school. Efforts here will be well repaid. The qualities of the tribe have so far mainly been used in opposition, but once put on the right lines the Kono could go far.

82. The tribe is the only matrilineal tribe in Kauru. (The Gure, along the hills in Lere District, are also a matrilineal society.) This does not, however, prevent marriage outside the tribe, usually with the Kitimi, who are an offshoot according to local history. There is no bride price among the Kono, except, amusingly enough, among some of those who have been to mission schools.

The Surubu

83. The Surubu were the first to descend from the hills. The Surubu range is smaller in extent than the Kauru hills although the main peak is higher. Gyshere, the main village, has a number of Hausa living in it and was originally a Hausa settlement on the trading route from the north to Zangon Katab. Many Surubu have adopted Islam and Hausa

dress and manners. The subvillage of Kabene is strongly Christian. It is interesting that despite the adoption of Islam the Surubu are most upset by the imposition of the *iddah* rule.

84. Cash crops are grown and cattle are owned. Development will probably be along Hausa lines.

85. There is a fine waterfall behind Gyshere. It is a pity that power sources are seldom where they are needed.

The Rishiwa

86. Though not in the hills the Rishiwa cannot be said to be in the plains. They farm an extensive valley in the foothills. Sleeping sickness is prevalent and takes a toll of energy. Of all the tribes they seemed the least lively, and there is open hostility between the young and old. The former complain that the latter do not want schools or any form of progress.

87. There is little cash-crop farming as yet.

The Kaibi

88. After the Ruruma and Kono the Kaibi are the most numerous and certainly the most energetic. Completely settled on the plain they have taken to cash crops and are good farmers. The chiefs are young and anxious to improve their lot. There are many literates but very few with formal schooling.

Other tribes

89. I was unable to visit the Dwingi, Kiballo, Kinuku, and Binawa. These are very small tribes, not more than two to three hundred in number, who live in single villages in the heart of the hills. There are also Kurama and Kadara in the very south of the district living in scattered hamlets between Lere and the river Kaduna. I hope to visit all these tribes shortly.

Proposals

90. I suggest the following proposals to develop the district. The hill peoples have for years been busy settling themselves on the plains without any help from government. Elsewhere large sums have been spent on settling people who did not want to be settled anyway. It seems only equitable that the Kauru tribes should receive some help even at this late stage.

(i) All village scribes to be appointed from the village in which they will work.

(ii) Local men to be appointed court scribes for Kwasam and Gyshere courts.

(iii) Three community schools to be built next year.
(iv) Adult literacy classes to be increased to twenty-five and a local organizer appointed.
(v) A co-operative assistant registrar to visit as soon as possible to encourage co-operative enterprise.
(vi) An agricultural officer to visit and if possible a production officer to be posted to it.
(vii) A wells team to go to the district.
(viii) Finally, and most important, the dry-season roads suggested in paragraph 32 to be built without delay.

91.   Several of these proposals require no expenditure and others are estimated for in a general way. The roads will require money and district council funds are insufficient. Development of Kauru could lead to a substantial increase in production and regional funds might therefore be available. Once we show that something is to be done in the district I am sure that it will be an excellent area for community development.

92.   It is a long time since this district was toured and there is much to do. I hope that I shall have the good fortune to do some of it. I have not toured before amid such scenic splendor, and I was much impressed by the potential of the area. More than anything else a firm lead is required. The most hopeful sign is the comparative success of the district council. Every encouragement should be given to it.

Zaria
25 Jan 54

Intelligence Report: Kauru and
Lere Districts

[Politics had become a factor in life, even for touring ADO's by 1954. We tended to avoid mention of political matters in open reports which would be read by Nigerians, a big change from a few years earlier. The Kano Annual Report for 1952, for example, even commented on the performance of Kano members in the House of Assembly! The Kauru hills were part of a general political problem in Zaria. I was anxious to get action and decided to play up the political angle, writing an intelligence report under secret cover to be read in conjunction with my touring notes on both Kauru and Lere districts.]

Politically the important matter is the relationship between the pagan peoples and the Hausa administration. The Hausa villages seem fairly happy, and Saminaka on the Bauchi Light Railway line is the only town with any number of Southerners. These are so busy making money that they have little time for politics and are ready to keep in with the DH in the usual manner.

2. The pagans, and especially those in the hills, feel very much neglected, as indeed they are. Mine was the first extensive administrative tour since 1938. Much has changed since then. By far the greater number of the people have moved to the plains and there has been a start in cash-crop farming. The social upheaval has been considerable and, unfortunately, the people have received very little help from outside. There is plenty of talent among the hill folk and they are adapting to their new way of life remarkably well. Malnutrition is common but standards are generally better than they were.

3. The Sudan Interior Mission at Gure has been the major outside influence. In Gure it has been too great, but elsewhere it has produced a number of literates who have taken the lead in descending from the hills and introducing cash crops. One of the material gains has been the art of sun-dried mud blocks, to which many of the tribes have taken with facility and skill. They are very ready to learn. It is a pity however that the only forms of Christianity so far presented have been extreme, namely the SIM and the Seventh-day Adventists.

4. Owing to the lack of cash crops many of the men seek dry-season

work, and the young men going to Jos, Kaduna, and Zaria have their eyes wide open. There is a high percentage of literacy, and adult classes are a great success.

5. Anti-Hausa feeling is widespread and often strong. Kauru, and not just the pagan area, has been much neglected by the NA. For example there is only one two-class school. The pagans see little for their taxes that is not abstract. There are a few wells and one dispensary. Otherwise they enjoy peace and are within thirty miles of the Bauchi Light. Consolation for some, it is not enough to prevent the belief that they are deliberately neglected by the Hausa NA. The main source of bitterness is over village scribes, all of whom are non-resident Hausa. The old excuse that nobody has the education is nonsense. In one village I found three boys with full senior primary education and fifty or more others literate. Village heads' sons were expressly put to school in Kauru so that they could become scribes, but nothing has been done to appoint them. Until the NA accepts that village scribes should be local men there will be no confidence in it, and the tribes will lack that sense of self-respect which is essential to well-being.

6. The young men know all about the proposals for southern Zaria and want to know why nothing is proposed for them. Most thought that Zonkwa was to become a separate division. I explained that they could not exist except in a larger grouping and that the natural line of communications from Kauru was north to Zaria rather than south to Zonkwa.

7. NEPU is strong, especially among the Ruruma, Kaibi, and Kono. I estimate some five hundred paying members. NEPU badges were on view at every village meeting. The people are good material for NEPU because of the lack of attention they have had from the NA and also because of the complete failure of the NPC to take any interest in the remoter areas. A NEPU badge indicates little, however. I found no bitterness against the British, everyone is intensely loyal to chiefs, and there is complete faith in the administration. They certainly don't toe the party line.

8. Most NEPU members are also members of the Middle Zone League, which is also supported by most of the Christians. Membership of both parties, which are not allied naturally, shows how little the game of politics is understood. The MZL is falling behind as it has no touring organization and attracts little national limelight.

9. At several villages I was asked to explain the NA Assemblies and Processions Rules. Unfortunately during my stay three NEPU men were fined £5 each for holding illegal meetings. I gather the Emir ordered their arrest during his tour. They are now martyrs, and one of them, Chindu Kwasam, has all the makings of a troublemaker.

10. Some young men, including NEPU members, expressed their fear

of self-government in 1956. They believe that the Hausa want self-government in order to keep the pagans under, and hope that the British will not depart until they are sufficiently advanced to look after their own interests. They point out that some of them were never really subject to the Hausa until after the British pacification patrols of 1907 and 1908. We have a special moral commitment to them.

11. Unless more attention is given to the area it will soon be politically dangerous. There are only some twenty thousand people all told, but they are united in their feeling against the Hausa, tempered only by the few who have adopted Islam and the need of the chiefs to toe the Hausa line in order to keep their office. There is time to remedy the situation, and my tour has helped the malcontents to get it off their chests as well as show them that they have not been entirely forgotten. Given self-respect and a lead the tribes will turn with a will to community development. In the midst of social upheaval if it is NEPU rather than government who is winning at present, the fault is with us.

12. There is absolutely no anti-European feeling. Indeed their faith in the ability of a young ADO to remedy all their ills was embarrassing. Everywhere my welcome was cordial and I have never toured among such friendly and well-mannered people. They could be a great asset to the province and the region, but they need help. I conclude with a remark made to me by a shrewd old man. He said that if Zaria NA did not want his people except as slaves they would be prepared to move right away. "We are in a period of transition and whether we decide to settle permanently near our old rocks or move right away will be our decision. The old men might stay, but the young would go." Highly improbable as this sounds it is not entirely inconceivable. Whether Kagoro, quoted as heaven on earth here, could cope with the influx is another matter.

Kauru
19 Jan 54

Index